Supervillains and Philosophy

Popular Culture and Philosophy®
Series Editor: George A. Reisch

For full details of all **Popular Culture and Philosophy**® books, visit www.opencourtbooks.com.

Popular Culture and Philosophy®

Supervillains and Philosophy

Sometimes, Evil Is Its Own Reward

Edited by
BEN DYER

OPEN COURT
Chicago and La Salle, Illinois

Volume 42 in the series, Popular Culture and Philosophy™, edited by George A. Reisch

To order books from Open Court, call toll-free 1-800-815-2280, or visit our website at www.opencourtbooks.com.

Open Court Publishing Company is a division of Carus Publishing Company.

Library of Congress Cataloging-in-Publication Data

Supervillains and philosophy / edited by Ben Dyer.
     p. cm.—(Popular culture and philosophy ; v. 42)
    Includes bibliographical references and index.
    ISBN-13: 978-0-8126-9669-1 (trade paper : alk. paper)
    1. Comic books, strips, etc.—Moral and ethical aspects.
  2. Villains in literature. I. Dyer, Ben, 1976-
    PN6712.S87 2009
    741.5'09—dc22
                                  2009021707

Contents

Phase Three
Taking Over the World   79

Phase Four
Beyond Good and Evil?   125

Phase Five
Fiendish Puzzles   157

Acknowledgments

There are many people who deserve thanks for helping make this book a reality. First, I'd like to thank David Ramsay Steele and series editor George Reisch for making this project possible. The volume's authors deserve special thanks for their brilliant toil under the cruel lash of the editor's pen. Libby Barringer deserves a special note of gratitude for an eleventh hour contribution that was both as brilliant as Ozymandias and as swift as Joker's usual stay in Arkham. I'm especially thankful for the contributions of our industry contributors John Ostrander and Denny O'Neil. Two nicer guys I could never hope to work with, and I hope you enjoy their chapters as much as I do.

On the home front, I wish to thank my wife, both for suggesting the possibility of doing this kind of volume, and for her continual support while I worked on it. A further note of thanks belongs to my friend Stuart Lowery for suggesting some helpful structural lines early on.

I'd also like to thank my parents for their special contributions without which this *particular* book might not have ever occurred. From my mother I learned to love language, reading, and writing. It was my father who bought me my first comic book, and it was also my father who had the moral rectitude to confiscate an issue of *Batman* so his young son would not see the Dark Knight say, "damn." I've been considering the moral qualities within comic books ever since.

Finally, to the industry professionals everywhere who continue to produce breathtaking art and amazing stories I am especially grateful—may the ink in your pens flow ever brightly.

The Devils Get Their Due

BEN DYER

I'm going to tell you the most important secret in modern comic books: the supervillains have won. It didn't happen in a massive battle that no one remembers, and it's not the result of hidden schemes concocted by secret puppet masters. It happened in comic shop conversations and writers' rooms in the 1970s and 1980s as the kids who'd started reading Silver Age comics in the Sixties began to grow up. As those kids' innocence gave way to adult maturity, they brought their funny books with them from childhood, and they forced their heroes to grow up too.

Green Lantern became socially conscious in the 1970s under Dennis O'Neil and Neal Adams, and Superman famously embarked on a "Quest for Peace" in the fourth and final movie featuring Christopher Reeve. This trend reached a watershed in the 1980s with the intensely layered psychology of Frank Miller's fanatical turn on Batman in *The Dark Knight Returns* (1986). A year later, Alan Moore had to invent *The Watchmen* because DC wouldn't let him take apart the characters they had just acquired from Charlton Comics. Since then, the *cri de coeur* of the comics *literati* is that our superheroes have feet of clay, and a sidelong glance at the heroes of the Silver Age reveals battle scars of an entirely different kind.

Batman is obsessive, manipulative, and emotionally closed off from even his closest companions. Green Lantern became the supervillain Parallax and tried to rewrite the history of the universe. Thor assumed the throne of Asgard and became a tyrant to humanity (for its own good of course). Our friendly neighborhood Spider-Man lost his one steady comfort in the world, his marriage to Mary Jane, in one of the most sweeping character rewrites comic fandom has ever seen. That would be bad enough, but the paragons of virtue in Marvel and DC comics have suffered the worst. When Superman returned to the silver screen in 2006, he was an absentee father who stalked Lois Lane at home with his x-ray vision. Captain America, the indomitable patriot and moral center of the Marvel Universe, is dead.

No supervillain ever accomplished so much. It had to be us.

It's obvious that supervillains haven't fared as poorly. On those infrequent occasions when they take center stage, supervillains are humanized and sympathetic, and they might have been us but for an untimely accident or mischance. Ah, but for an unfortunate turn, these same madmen, murderers, and masterminds might even have been superheroes! After all, doesn't Magneto just want to protect mutantkind, and isn't Ra's Al Ghul just trying to save the planet? Lex Luthor is just a frustrated humanist, and if he troubles himself to remember the names of his janitor's kids, he can't be all bad, can he?

That the supervillains are now barely distinct from their superheroic counterparts is a criminal lapse in judgment, but the source of that important mistake is quite subtle. Stan Lee once said that the most important character in any comic is the supervillain.

> Want proof? Let's take just one example. Where would Spider-Man be without the Green Goblin, Doc Ock, the Lizard, the Sandman, the Kingpin, or any of his other splendidly savage and sinister supervillains? Sure, you always need the hero, but ask yourself this: how eager would you be to read about a superhero who fought litterbugs, jaywalkers, or income-tax evaders? (*The Supervillain Book: The Evil Side of Comics and Hollywood*, Gina Misiroglu and Michael Eury eds.)

Stan's exactly right that each and every villain in the superhero's rogues gallery should be as formidable a challenge as the hero's powers are extraordinary. But it's not the powers that make someone a hero, it's the character beneath the cowl. The same is true of supervillains. Today's supervillains wield powers and abilities that make them every bit the superhero's equal in physical power, but where is the moral or existential challenge to match the modern superhero's new psychology? Tragically, there is very little contrast left between the moral cynicism of modern narratives and the sympathetic lens through which we encounter the modern supervillain.

Well, let those who worship evil's might beware our scholars' keen insight!

It's time for the devils to get their due. In this volume we're going to take apart the supervillains. We'll analyze the monologues and the madness, and we'll put the masterminds in check. We'll consider the supervillain's life, his or her relation to morality and society, and the intellectual boundaries and puzzles that keep us interested in these most important of comic book characters.

Is a little tyranny justified in the pursuit of a good cause? If someone finally became all-powerful, is there anything they couldn't do? Can someone truly desire evil? Why the heck are good henchmen so hard to find? We'll tackle these questions in the pages to come, and we'll rediscover the contrasts that set our favorite heroes apart from their arch-nemeses.

If you think the hard light of modern literary sensibilities has already shown us the cracks and flaws in our favorite heroes, wait until you see what it does to the villains.

Phase One

So You Want to Be a Supervillain . . .

1

The Wandering Unwanted

BEN DYER

What happens when the scales fall from your eyes and the real clock-work of the world is laid bare? What happens when you're Wesley Gibson, one minute the most downtrodden wretch the world has ever seen, and the next . . . you're Wanted?

Stop me if you've heard this one: your life is an unmitigated train wreck of failure on top of failure; your career is a dead end street paved with everyone else's expectations, and you know beyond a certainty that you're a disappointment to your friends, family, and ultimately (and worst of all) to yourself. You are walked on, spit on, cheated on (assuming someone will go out with you), laughed at, and miserable.

Here's the icing on the cake. What makes you *really* pathetic is that you've internalized the whole thing. You check the Internet to see which disease is almost certainly eating you from the inside out, and you pop a pharmacy of pills just in case. You put up with your boss's overbearing micromanagement even though she's got no more idea how to do your job than her stapler has. Your friends take advantage of the pathetic fact that you'll *never* say no because they know you're not *capable* of standing up for yourself. You're now your own worst critic and you think you *deserve* all this.

If you think that story's familiar, then you've probably been reading *Wanted* by Mark Millar, J.G. Jones, and Paul Mounts. This is Wesley Gibson's story, or at least the start of his story, and what happens next may sound like a dream come true. Into his life walks Fox, a smokin' hot woman (you can pick Hallie or Angelina) with the word that his deadbeat absentee father died, leaving him more money than he could ever spend. Wait, that's not the best part. Even better is the fact that he's now entitled to live a life without consequences. "You can shoot, kill, rape, or destroy anyone you like now, baby," Fox smiles, "consequences are for the little people when you got a seat in the Fraternity."

The Fraternity she's referring to are the world's collected supervillains, carefully hidden from public view, who run *everything* because they finally managed to rid themselves of interference from the world's superheroes. If that sounds decidedly unliterary, then you've not been thinking very carefully about what happens when every superhero's got a rogues gallery of five or ten more supervillains. One at a time they're manageable maybe, but Wesley learns from Professor Solomon Seltzer, one of the five supervillains who divided the world when the dust settled, that

> Supervillains just got tired of getting beaten all the time and so we started scheming in our prison cells and secret headquarters. We just devised a plan unlike any we'd ever tried before . . . We decided to work as a team. Not just the ten or twelve supervillains that made up each of these rogue galleries and such, but the hundreds and thousands of super-criminals all across the planet. Individually we'd always failed to make much impact, but as an army I hypothesized we'd be pretty much unbeatable. The final battle took place in 1986. It lasted almost three months and we lost a great many friends during that encounter, but we beat them in the end. By the middle of August, there wasn't a superhero left standing from one end of this globe to the other.

Wesley's new life is the one recently vacated by his absentee father, the Killer, the world's greatest hitman, and the best part is that he can do *anything he wants*. Want to get even with anyone who's ever pissed you off? Check. How about the rush of "blowing holes in men of steel and slitting the throats of dark-night detectives?" Absolutely. That kind of power is a heady draft, and it transforms Wesley from "the most insignificant asshole of the twenty-first century" into The (new) Killer. Thus intoxicated and released from the insignificance of his former life, he can finally say, "f*** you Mom. F*** you all those teachers who said I was too lazy to ever amount to anything."[1]

---

[1] No, this essay wasn't censored by the publisher. I just don't have Mark Millar's potty mouth. Besides, if you were me you'd know your mother *is* reading this. What's wrong with you?

Wanted is the story where the devils finally get their due, and that's what this book is about, giving supervillains their due. Herein you'll find all the mad scientists and world-conquerors, the misguided idealists and the raving lunatics, and some *really* smart people thinking about their lives, choices, and reasons. I'll leave you to find your favorite villain elsewhere if it's not Wesley Gibson, but *Wanted* is an especially pure example of the breed because there's not a superhero in sight.

Wanted has no redeeming moment where the superheroes suddenly save the world at the end. There's not even a reflective *dénouement* where the supervillain's crown sits heavily on Wesley Gibson's untouchable head. The book appears remorseless (though you'll see that's not quite true), and two things occurred to me when I first read it. First, Wesley reminded me of another person—an apparently quite ordinary person—who saw his life as a failure until he was swept up into an eerily similar firmament of intoxicating power. I'll just call him "Mr. E," and note that yes, that name *would be* an unforgivable pun (say it out loud, kids) if "E" wasn't *actually* the initial letter of his last name. People like Mr. E scare the hell out of me, and they're as real as the book in your hands, but we'll get to him a bit later.

The second thing Wesley's story reminded me of was that old metaphor in Plato's *Republic* about the cave. Plato once ruled philosophy the way the dinosaurs ruled the primordial earth. He was one of the first, he was one of the biggest, and everybody that came afterward starts telling the historical story by studying the footprints he left. That's partly because Plato bequeathed to all subsequent Western history the idea that, like Wesley's world in *Wanted*, there's a more basic world, a *truer* world than the one pulled over our eyes. That's what the cave is about in Book 7 of the *Republic*,

> Imagine human beings living in an underground, cavelike dwelling, with an entrance a long way up, which is both open to the light and as wide as the cave itself. They've been there since childhood, fixed in the same place, with their necks and legs fettered, able to see only in front of them, because their bonds prevent them from turning their heads around. Light is provided by a fire burning far above and behind them. Also behind them, but on higher ground, there is a path stretching between them and the fire. Imagine that along this a low wall has been built, like the screen in front of the puppeteers above which they show their puppets . . . there are people along the wall, carrying all

kinds of artifacts that project above it—statues of people and other animals . . . prisoners see [nothing] of themselves [or] one another besides the shadows that the fire casts on the wall in front of them . . .

Can you see it in your head? Can you imagine the iron shackles and the darkness? In those bonds, in that darkness, Plato's prisoners can't see anything but the shadowplay on the dimly lit cave wall directly in front of their eyes, *and they think that's reality*. Then, just like Wesley Gibson, one of them gets free from the constraints of his former life and gets his eyes opened. One of the prisoners finally discovers the world behind the shadowplay, as he leaves his chains behind and walks in the dazzling light of day. In Plato's thought, what that light illuminates is knowledge, and the painful upward climb—the excruciating act of seeing itself—is the work of philosophy and the philosopher.

Like Wesley Gibson, we all start like those prisoners in the dark; but Wesley Gibson is no philosopher, and there are darker regions in Plato's cave. Keep that in mind as we go, because we're about to meet someone who wanders there.

Dark Parallels

It's time for me to tell you about Mr. E. He's an individual whose life bears some eerie resemblances to Wesley Gibson's. Like Wesley, Mr. E's early career was a steady chain of failures. His father removed him from a spectacularly unremarkable high school career so he could be even more disappointing in vocational school. His father likewise used his connections to get him his first job as a salesman, and his uncle did the same with his second. He was fired from the latter in the Spring of 1933, and like Wesley Gibson, he probably thought, "I'm not a bad person or anything. I'm just an ordinary guy in a *bad situation* . . ." Like Wesley Gibson, he was soon after inducted into an evil fraternity.

Unlike Wesley Gibson, he almost got away with it.

I'll introduce you to him again, later in life, his dark deeds done. It's 6:30 P.M. on May 11th, 1960, and a bus deposits him in a poor suburb on the outskirts of Buenos Aires. He makes his home there in a primitive brick house with no electricity or running water. The papers in his pocket identify him as Ricardo Klement, an Italian national who now resides in Argentina on a work permit. He works at the Mercedes-Benz factory. His star has certainly fallen, but he still walks free and lives with his family. I know relatively little about his wife and four children, but so far as I know, after 6:30 P.M. they never see him alive again.

As Klement steps off the bus, he's seized by three men and hustled into a car that takes him to a rented room outside the city. A doctor examines him there, and he is interrogated by his captors. He stays in that room until he's spirited out of the country eight days later, and his destination is the state of Israel. He will be tried for crimes against the Jewish people and against all of humanity for his role in the Holocaust. Because I told you that Mr. E's name is no pun, you've probably guessed that those papers in Ricardo Klement's pocket are false. Mr. E's real name is Otto Adolf Eichmann, *Obersturmbannführer a.D.* in Adolf Hitler's S.S.[2]

I won't rehearse Eichmann's career in the S.S. because there's nothing really interesting about desk work. Eichmann never failed to be the cog that Wesley once was. He was a bureaucrat, not a hitman, and most of the time that's what supervillainy looks like in real life. Eichmann's on trial in Jerusalem because he's the logistical mastermind behind the trains and the death-camps. The former ran on time, and the latter were a marvel of ghastly efficiency. Yes, if you're paying attention to their day jobs, Wesley is nothing like Eichmann. But there are other parallels and I think they're disturbing enough.

Eichmann shares with Wesley Gibson a very specific pattern of motivation, and a very specific response to the moral burdens of his new life. Here's what Hannah Arendt says about Eichmann's attitude toward his life while on trial in Jerusalem:

> From a humdrum life without significance and consequence the wind had blown him into History . . . [though] he never forgot what the alternative would have been. Not only in Argentina, leading the unhappy existence of a refugee, but also in the courtroom in Jerusalem, with his life as good as forfeited, he might still have preferred—if anybody had asked him—to be hanged as *Obersturmbannführer a.D.* (in retirement)

---

[2] The details of this account are taken mainly from Hannah Arendt's *Eichmann in Jerusalem: A Report on the Banality of Evil* (Penguin, 1964). Arendt was no fan of Plato's claim that there was a more fundamental world of forms or ideas behind the world of experience. Yet if she and Plato had read *Wanted*, they probably would have agreed that Wesley's and Eichmann's lives were failures to begin with—and became worse—because they were "unexamined lives" as Socrates liked to say.

rather than living out his life quietly and normally as a traveling salesman for the Vacuum Oil Company. (*Eichmann in Jerusalem*, pp.
33–34)

The failed career and the humdrum life motivate Eichmann to join
something that gives his life "significance," and he never looks
back. Maybe because he's not being asked to do desk work,
Wesley takes a little longer. In the movie, Wesley's training isn't finished until the Repairman beats it out of him that he doesn't know
who he is. In the comics Wesley discovers he's found his life's work
as he kills "people who pissed me off as a kid" while working his
way up to cops and superheroes from parallel dimensions. It does-
n't happen overnight though, and that's the second point of similarity: for both Wesley and Eichmann their first victim is conscience.

When Eichmann learned of the Final Solution—the physical
extermination of the Jews—he confessed that he "lost everything,
all joy in my work, all initiative, all interest; I was, so to speak,
blown out" (p. 84). When he visited the camps, he couldn't stand
to actually watch the bloody work he ordered others to do. As the
qualms of his troubled conscience raised their voice, Eichmann
faced a choice. He could kill his conscience or he could kill his
career. You already know he did the former, but the *how* is worth
mentioning. Like many others, Eichmann convinced himself that
he was doing something *good*. Implementing the Final Solution
was a matter of national interest during a time of war, and he *had*
to set aside his own personal feelings on the matter. And so, from
a desk job in Hitler's Third Reich, Adolf Eichmann killed his conscience by absolving himself of the responsibility to disobey the
orders issued by his superiors, telling himself all the while that
those internal pangs were a noble burden in a great and noble
enterprise.

Wesley also makes that choice, but he's not nearly so squea-
mish. Wesley spends the first weeks of his new life killing random
strangers and slaughtering animals. He explains that,

> The reason I'm doing fourteen days in a slaughterhouse here is to get
> me as numb and desensitized as your average eight-year-old. I'm a
> friend of the Earth, a Greenpeace campaigner, and a vegetarian of
> some eleven years standing you understand. That's a s***-load of
> empathy I need to get rid of, but three calves a minute seems a pretty
> good place to start.

Only once does Wesley ever voice doubt. Three months into his new life he passes a police precinct and, with nothing better to do, decides to stop and kill every cop inside. All except "some lady cop in her forties who was downstairs watching the cells . . . she was just some scrawny mom with baggy eyes and corn rows." There amid the carnage, with the inmates cheering him on, he breaks down into tears before leaving to find Fox. She plies him with sex, drugs, and alcohol, and once his mood's "settled," he has a reflective moment. He muses, "I didn't know those cops from Adam, but I still walked in and used my powers to ruin their families' lives, right?" Wesley starts to wonder if "maybe this 'being evil all the time' crap's starting to feel a little forced," but Fox reassures him that

> You don't have time to rape, kill, and mutilate people all the time, baby. Your dad wasn't trying to turn you into the biggest sociopath that ever walked the Earth. He just wanted you to do what you really wanted with your life and sometimes that means watching TV in bed all day long and other times it's murdering some f***er. The whole point of this exercise was to bring a little choice into that sad, pathetic thing you used to call your life.

Did you catch that sleight-of-hand? Fox's doesn't even answer the question. Instead, she *bribes* Wesley to kill off the last embers of his conscience by presenting him with a choice. It's not a choice between good and evil, but between the free pleasures of his new life and the self-loathing conformity of his old life. When she puts it that way, Wesley's ambitions blind him to the fact that it's a false dilemma. You can be certain that if Fox thought for one second that Wesley's ideal was neither of those things, but (oh, for instance) to start standing for Truth, Justice, and the American Way because of the great responsibility that came with his great power, she'd ice him without a second thought. Fox's ideal is the enjoyment and maintenance of the supervillains' secret global empire, and she murdered her conscience in its service long ago.

So that's how the last light of Wesley's conscience goes out. It's smothered by a messenger wreathed in pot-smoke, drenched in sex and alcohol, whose message is freedom from consequence. Three months in, Wesley is so far gone that it doesn't even count as temptation. Had Eichmann known Wesley, he might have recognized a fellow traveler if he wasn't appalled by Wesley's hedonism. Had

Wesley known Eichmann, he might have learned that Fox was lying about something really important. There is at least one consequence of Wesley's choices that even the Fraternity cannot cover up, and they knew it even *before* their climactic battle with the superheroes in 1986.

Dark Choices, Darker Costs

Something happens when you kill your conscience, and Wesley might have understood this as Arendt did had he been present when Eichmann uttered his last words at the gallows.

> He began by stating emphatically that he was a *Gottgläubiger*, to express in common Nazi fashion that he was no Christian and did not believe in life after death. He then proceeded: "After a short while, gentlemen, *we shall meet again*. Such is the fate of all men. Long live Germany, long live Argentina, long live Austria. *I shall not forget them.*" In the face of death, he had found the cliché used in funeral oratory. Under the gallows, his memory played him the last trick; he was "elated" and he forgot that this was his own funeral. It was as though in those last minutes he was summing up the lesson that this long course in human wickedness had taught us—the lesson of the fearsome, word-and-thought-defying *banality of evil.* (p. 252)

It wasn't just conscience that Eichmann and the supervillains of the Fraternity had lost. It was a certain kind of *connection to reality*. Eichmann's testimony was a morass of clichés and sepia-toned half-memories utterly disconnected from the suffering he'd caused. Not even the finality of the gallows could restore him to reality because he'd *willingly* destroyed that connection in his own conscience. In his final moments, he never realized that when conscience goes missing, it takes with it some ineffable texture or tone that gives us insight into ourselves, our relationships, and our world.

Remember when I said that the book wasn't *quite* remorseless? In the its closing moments we get a second supervillain's perspective on the fateful days prior to the apocalyptic battle in the Summer of 1986.

> The sky was so blue in those days . . . The trees were a deeper green than you can possibly imagine and the food was so rich and tasty compared to that s*** you eat today. There was a moment we almost didn't go ahead with the revolution we'd been planning. A moment we

didn't want to let things go all grim and gritty . . . But it was only for a moment . . . By morning, all the magic in the world was gone and your mother thought your father had been an airline pilot.

When you choose to live without consequences, what you get is an inconsequential life. That's the one consequence the Fraternity cannot cover up. Once you've killed the part of your soul that knows the difference between what matters and what doesn't, nothing can matter to you *ever again*. That's the hidden irony of *Wanted*, that in spite of the fact that Wesley gets "the girl, the cash, and [ends] our story as one of the secret masters of the world," it can't be worth anything to him. He can choose any and all of it in any amount he wants, but because he's "as numb and desensitized as your average eight-year-old," he'll never actually value *any* of it.

This should bother you if you've still got Plato's cave in mind. Wesley's ambition leads him out of the shackles of his pathetic former life, but it likewise leads him to destroy a basic part of his connection to the world. Wesley discovers a more fundamental world than the one he knew, just as Plato predicted he would. But Plato predicts a world of light and knowledge, where we experience and value the world as it *truly* is. Wesley's world is a darker place, and to get there he must blind and desensitize himself.

Wanted follows Wesley's progress from the moment he slips the bonds of his old life to the moment he embraces final darkness by killing the most important part of his soul. If Wesley's journey began in Plato's cave, he may well have gone far from the light of the fire, but he did not go up to the world of light and knowledge. Instead, he *descended further* from the world of knowledge and value by surrendering his conscience and leaving behind what dim light he had. In that darkness I imagine he'll wander endlessly without light enough find his way back, and the sad irony is that he won't even realize he's lost. But at least he's not alone. Eichmann wandered there, and though I can't tell you what things wander in that darkness now, I do know they are all the more pitiable for having left the dim light of the fire.

2
Why Good Help Is Hard to Find

RON NOVY

and the stony-hearted villains know it well enough:
a plague upon it when thieves cannot be true one to another!

—FALSTAFF, in *Henry IV, Part 1*

Something has gone terribly wrong—again. Your devilishly-clever plan to corner the international trade in processed dairy products has been foiled by some do-gooder wearing his underpants on the outside of his brightly-colored tights. World domination has been ripped from your fingers, no thanks to your bumbling lackeys. The county lock-up is even now filling with members of your gang. And so, *again* you'll need to keep a low profile, *again* you'll defer claiming your rightful title of "Big Cheese, World's Most Super Colossal Stupendous Villain," and *again* you'll need to place a few discrete "henchmen wanted" ads. This time you mean it: no clowns, no idiots, no psychopaths, and no blabbermouths.

The police are no doubt well into the interrogation of your now-former lieutenants Muenster and Feta, grilling them under bright lights in a bare room. Even now, Officer Good Cop is offering Henchman Muenster immunity from prosecution if he will reveal the next phase of your master plan, while Officer Bad Cop is promising Henchman Feta that he will never again see the light of day unless he reveals the location of your secret lair. As a top-shelf baddie, you are elegantly brutal: a master of evil sleight of hand, brilliant at humiliating superheroes, and feared throughout the underworld—why else would they call you *"The* Big Cheese?" Nonetheless, even a criminal mastermind can have trust issues. Can your henchmen be trusted to keep your secrets? After all, to do so

13

will likely commit them to an extended visit upstate to the world of orange jumpsuits, cavity searches, and nutraloaf. Whether or not you can trust your henchmen not to rat on you to Johnny Law will depend in part upon what sort of relationship exists between you and your henchmen: Are they friends, hired help, or something else all together?

Calling All Caseophiles

> For no one would choose to live without friends even if he had all other goods.
>
> —ARISTOTLE (*Nicomachean Ethics* 1155a5)

Trust is an essential aspect of friendship, and it was Aristotle who made one of the earliest efforts to sort out just what it is to be a friend. While we today generally limit the term "friendship" to close relationships existing between ourselves and a select few acquaintances, for Aristotle "friendship" is something much more broad. Aristotle's "friends" would include family members, business associates, and drinking buddies—just about anybody with whom he was at all familiar. Friendship exists for Aristotle whenever there is "a mutual attraction between two human beings."[1] In *Nicomachean Ethics,* Aristotle describes three distinct sorts of friendships: those of utility, those of pleasure, and those between "good people similar in virtue" (lines 1156b 6–7). These relationships are less points on a spectrum than differences in fundamental composition—that is, differences not in the quantity units on some mysterious "buddy-o-meter," but in the quality and durability of the relationship.

The most common sort of friendship discussed by Aristotle is one based in utility: that is, one in which the friends each receive some practical benefit from the relationship. The relationships between a barkeep and his patrons, between members of a professional lawn bowlers association, or between a roofer and the owner of the leaking house are often friendships of this sort. A friendship of utility lasts so long as the mutual benefits continue. Thus, so long as your supervillain brains and your henchman's brawn continue to complement one another, the two of you are friends.

---

[1] See David Ross's *Aristotle* (Routledge, 1995), p. 235

Such relationships can be thought of as a simple economic exchange: you provide Henchman Havarti a wage; she provides her service as a get-away driver. For Aristotle, this friendship between you as a supervillain and Havarti as henchman is "incomplete" due to its temporary nature: the relationship will end once you no longer require a driver, Henchman Havarti is hired away by another supervillain, or the job—say, looting a local savings and loan—is completed.

For Aristotle, there's a second, less common sort of "incomplete friendship" based on pleasure instead of utility. So imagine that you and Gun Moll Gruyère carry on a torrid affair or at least that the two of you meet once a week for cribbage and a sandwich; in either case, you would be friends of this second sort. As with the utility-based friendship, a friendship based on pleasure continues only so long as that mutual enjoyment continues. Thus, the Big Cheese–Gun Moll Gruyère friendship may end when she takes up with the barely villainous Breadmaster or when either of you loses the taste for cribbage. Together, friendships of utility and friendships of pleasure account for nearly all of our friendships.

The rarest and most laudable sort of friendship—what Aristotle calls "perfect" or "complete" friendship—is one in which the friends "wish goods to their friend for the friend's own sake" (lines 1156b 9–10). Reportedly Aristotle characterized complete friendship as "one soul abiding in two bodies"[2]—an extension of one's own love of self to include another. According to David Ross, when Aristotle refers to individuals "treating their friends as 'other selves' . . . he is pointing to the fact that a man may so extend his interests that the welfare of another may become as direct an object of interest to him as his own welfare" (p. 237).

A perfect friendship is thus "other-focused," for the friend identifies her friend's interests as her own and wishes only the best for her friend for the friend's own sake. As Aristotle puts it,

> Decent people . . . are in concord with themselves and with each other, since they are practically of the same mind; for their wishes are stable, not flowing back and forth like a tidal strait. . . . Base people, however, cannot be in concord, except to a small extent, just as they can be friends only to a small extent, for they are greedy for more

---

[2] See Diogenes Laertius. *Lives and Opinions of Eminent Philosophers*, Book V, part XI.

benefits, and shirk labors and public services. (*Nichomachean Ethics*, lines 1167b 5–12)

Virtue then is an essential trait of complete friendship. Thus, for Aristotle there is an intimate connection between "friendship" and "the good life." It turns out, that the reverse is also true—that complete friendship is also a necessary condition for living a virtuous life.

For Aristotle, people cannot be happy without friends. He believes that the function of a human being is to attain happiness, and since we are the sorts of creatures "tending by nature to live with others," part of that function includes living well with others (lines 1097a15–b21 and 1169b18–19). This is, in part, what he means when he says that "man is by nature a political animal."[3] In short, we require others in order to function fully within our nature, for "friendship seems to consist more in loving than in being loved" (line 1159a27).

Do Rats Like Cheese?

You of course are Big Cheese—a supervillain without equal (though on occasion fortune has smiled on some masked boy scout in your encounters and you've agreed to disagree on the "without equal" matter with other so-called supervillains). So let's suppose that the police detectives are interrogating Henchman Muenster and Henchman Feta. What sort of friendship might you have with them? Will they betray you? More importantly, is that bond strong enough to prevent their betrayal?

It seems reasonable to suggest that Muenster and Feta are friends of the most basic sort to Big Cheese. Along with the other members of the gang—Henchmen Jarlsberg and Stilton, *femme fatale* Camembert de Normandie, and the fallen clergyman known only as the Stinking Bishop—they receive training and payment, have access to your hideaway cottage in Kurdistan, have their costuming needs met, and beef-up their bad guy résumés by their mere association with Big Cheese. In return, Big Cheese minimally gets the labor and skills needed to execute his plans for global dairy domination. Such a network of utility friendships can be expected to continue so long as it is of reciprocal benefit to all parties involved.

---

[3] See Aristotle's *Politics*, I.1253a2.

As mentioned earlier, it's certainly possible that some of the friendships Big Cheese has with his henchmen could be—or at least could approach—friendships of pleasure. There is of course the physical pleasure of being around those one finds physically attractive (Aristotle does place romantic relations in this category of friendships), but there may also be pleasure in the shared risk of a job, the adrenaline rush of fleeing the police, and the celebratory toasts down at Happy Harry's following your success. While transitory like utility friendships, it is at least possible that Big Cheese has this sort of pleasure-based friendship with some of his henchmen.

Consider the friendship between Big Cheese and his right-hand man, Roquefort. They have primarily a utility friendship. Even if—thanks to his supervillain-sized temper—the position of "right hand man" is often in need of urgent refilling, Roquefort himself gives respect and authority to Big Cheese and keeps the rest of the henchmen in line. In return, Roquefort receives some part of the gang's wealth, the ability to exercise power over the "lesser" henchmen, and possibly even the respect of his fellow gangsters. If Roquefort's relationship with Big Cheese entails something like an apprentice-master relation, the pleasures of learning on one hand and of teaching on the other may even elevate this utility-based relationship into something approaching a "friendship of pleasure."

Similarly, we can imagine that if the relationship between Gun Moll Gruyère and Big Cheese took a romantic turn, they too may succeed in pushing their henchman-to-supervillain friendship of utility into something more like a friendship of pleasure.

However, it seems unlikely that Big Cheese's relation with either Roquefort or with Gruyere could ever be sustained as a friendship of pleasure. The pleasure received by either henchman would always be restricted by the inability to fully trust Big Cheese, just as his pleasure would be limited by the inability to trust either of his underlings. After all, no supervillain would entrust his deepest secrets to another if he expects to remain in the supervillain game for very long. Big Cheese's henchmen no doubt aspire to greater villainhood and would undoubtedly be willing to step over Big Cheese's corpse to get it. Similarly, both Gun Moll Gruyère and Right Hand Roquefort recognize that they are disposable and replaceable within the Big Cheese criminal organization. As such, they too must withhold some part of themselves in their friendships with Big Cheese. The lack of mutual trust restricts the bounds of their friendship so that in the end, both must see their relationship with Big Cheese as one of utility with a few laughs along the way.

Needless to say, Big Cheese and his henchmen also can never have something like a complete friendship given their hierarchical relationship as well as the well-known supervillain penchant for self-absorption and instinct for self-preservation. If Big Cheese took to heart the interests of another and promoted these as ends in themselves, he simply could not show his face at the annual convention of the International Guild of Scoundrels, Knaves, and Villains.

Is It Labor at the Wheel?

Unbecoming to a gentleman, too, and vulgar are the means of livelihood of all hired workmen whom we pay for mere manual labor, not for artistic skill; for in their case the very wage they receive is a pledge of their slavery.

—CICERO, *De Officiis*, Book 1 XLII

Within the context of Aristotelian friendship, it seems Big Cheese can only count on the strength of his utility-based friendships with Henchman Feta and Henchman Muenster to keep them from rolling over under police interrogation. Such a relationship can never supply the level of trust a supervillain would require of his henchmen. Yet, as we're talking about turning state's evidence against not just any gangster, but against a supervillain like Big Cheese, perhaps loyalty could be expected if the relationship were understood not as a form of friendship, but instead as something like employment without the bothersome niceties of OSHA regulation or Social Security withholdings.

After all, Big Cheese makes arrangements with his henchmen that appear to be the kind of wage labor with which most of us are familiar. An employee provides some service or labor to the employer, and in exchange the employer compensates the employee with a paycheck. However, appearances can be deceiving. The employment relation is a contractual one, and contracts require some sort of recognized social structure which can enforce the terms of the contract. Such legal recourse is quite difficult to come by for a criminal enterprise. So, while Big Cheese's arrangements resemble employment, in fact they are not. Instead, the relationship would be better understood as something more like that of a pirate crew: self-interested individuals who band together around a captain in order to gain from endeavors which would be impossible to undertake individually.

Health Hazards in Natural Cheese

In *Leviathan*, Thomas Hobbes describes "the state of nature"—the condition in which humanity found itself prior to coming together in civil society: a time without cheesecakes, cheese fondue, cheese balls, and cheesy poofs. "During this time, men live without a common power to keep them all in awe, they are in that condition which is called war—a war of every man against every man."[4]

As there is no society (and so no legal system) to which people can appeal, each person has what Hobbes calls a natural right to do whatever she deems necessary to preserve and benefit her own safety, liberty, and life. Given that all of us share more or less the same needs and desires, and given that the available resources to fulfill those needs and desires are scarce, life in the state of nature is famously "solitary, poor, nasty, brutish, and short."

Beginning with this horrible scenario, Hobbes appeals to our shared desire to live peaceably and our shared fear of death to serve as the basis for civil governance. Consenting parties enter into a contractual relation under which they exchange their natural rights for a set of life-preserving rules and a sovereign who enforces those rules. For Hobbes, this arrangement is what enables humanity to escape from this war of all against all into what we recognize as civil society.

Muenster, Roquefort, the Stinking Bishop, and the rest lack just such an enforcer for their arrangements, and so "natural right" is always lurking just below the surface. The henchmen—like the pirate crew—may revolt anytime they judge that their best interests are not being served. Like the pirate captain, at any time Big Cheese may judge that his interests are not being met appropriately and so abuse the henchmen—be it by simply skimming a little off of the top for himself or by framing a certain Mr. Bleu in order to keep Z.O.W.I.E., U.N.C.L.E., and MI6 off of his trail.

It's the Second Mouse that Gets the Cheese

Before Hobbes leads our imagined ancestors into civilization, he does discuss some of the available strategies for survival within the

---

[4] See Thomas Hobbes, *Leviathan* (Oxford University Press, 1998), p. 84.

state of nature. One—"*modus vivendi*," (literally, "way of living")—closely matches our henchmen-supervillain situation.[5] What Hobbes describes is a consensus based on pragmatic self-interest that permits individuals to band together to bring about some desirable end that is individually unachievable. The stability of the *modus vivendi* endures so long as the parties find that their individual interests are being served. Cicero reminds us of the internal operating rules necessary for such an agreement:

> For if a robber takes anything by force or by fraud from another member of the gang, he loses his standing even in a band of robbers; and if the one called the "Pirate Captain" should not divide the plunder impartially, he would be either deserted or murdered by his comrades. Why, they say that robbers even have a code of laws to observe and obey. (Cicero, *De Officiis*, Book II, xi–xii, Section XI)

This "code" holds so long as the individual highwaymen deem it to be worth their while; when it is found to not be in their individual interests—as when the "pirate captain" fails to divvy the loot appropriately—we see individuals abandon the code.

The problem with any "code of law" agreed to under the *modus vivendi* is that it lacks a principled foundation (say, a concept of justice or of rights). Thus, any party to it—if she believes she can do better at the expense of the others—can as easily withdraw her consent from the agreement in order to pursue her individual interest. It is possible to imagine that the *modus vivendi* agreement is even more fragile than that since to even suspect that there is a possibility of another party cheating is a justification to pre-emptively betray others before being betrayed oneself.

The possibility that one party will see some advantage in the betrayal of the others is the 800-pound gorilla of an otherwise stable *modus vivendi* agreement, and that's why there's a good chance that the cops are on their way to your lair right now. Feta and Muenster have been offered a choice: to stick with an unenforceable code and accept the state's punishment or to pursue their individual interests by revealing Big Cheese's secret Green Bay hideaway.

---

[5] While not used by Hobbes, the term is used in John Rawls's analysis of the Hobbesian state of nature in *Political Liberalism* (Columbia University Press, 1996).

What Curdles the Blood

Often we find that when individuals act for their particular interests, no one is the recipient of optimal results, and all parties may come to a disastrous end. In *Laches*, Plato offers an early example of how just such a thing can come to pass in his discussion of a soldier at the Battle of Delium.[6] A soldier reasons that if his side's position holds against the enemy assault, his personal involvement in repulsing the attack will be negligible. Since staying at the barricade puts him at risk while offering little to the defense, there seems to be good reason for him to abandon his post. On the other hand, were the enemy's assault to overwhelm the defensive position, the chance of the soldier's death or injury are even greater; again the soldier has good reason to abandon his post. Therefore, regardless of how the clash plays out, it seems to be in the soldier's best interest to flee.

Of course, each of the Athenian defenders is as rational and self-interested as the first soldier and will have similarly recognized that fleeing is in his individual interest as well. This realization reinforces each soldier's desire to flee since no one of their number can hold the position alone. In this way, each follows his individual interest, each abandons the position, and each is killed or captured by the attacking Boeotian army. Yet, were they to stand together to repel the attackers, not only would more of them survive, but they would retain control of the resources that would otherwise be lost.

If Big Cheese's trust in his henchmen is not due to either the love we find in a complete friendship or to the limited benefits of a pragmatic *modus vivendi* agreement, how is it that he has any confidence that neither Feta nor Muenster will "abandon the line" in the face of Johnny Law's best efforts?

In *Henry V* (Act VI, Scene VI)—just as the English efforts have begun to flag at the Battle of Agincourt—Shakespeare offers us a possible response. While not usually characterized as a villain by anyone other than the French of his day, King Harry surprises his officers by ordering the execution of their prisoners within sight of the French lines. The English soldiers know that because the French have witnessed the slaughter, no mercy can be expected if

---

[6] This battle of the Peloponnesian War in 424 B.C.E. concluded with a siege by Boeotian forces of an Athenian force at Delium. Alcibiades, who appears in several Socratic dialogues, is said to have rescued Socrates during the Athenian retreat.

they fall into French hands. King Harry's execution order changed the expectations of soldiers on both sides: instilling a fear of the English brutality in the French while instilling in the English the knowledge that the only chance of surviving the battle is to win it. With this action, King Harry prevents the mass desertions predicted by Plato because fleeing sacrifices the English soldiers' only chance of surviving Agincourt.

Like King Harry, Big Cheese may be able to insure his henchmen's loyalty despite the interrogating detectives' threats and promises – he can leave them no choice. Just as the English soldiers had only the options of death or maintaining their loyalty to the English cause, Henchmen Feta and Muenster must be made to see their options are also loyalty or death (or possibly something worse than death, since unlike King Harry, Big Cheese *is* a supervillain). A supervillain has the capacity to make a credible threat against any person, her family, her friends, and her pets. It is merely a matter of how creatively Big Cheese completes the sentence: "If you betray me …" To paraphrase W.C. Fields, "A clever cat eats cheese and breathes down the rat hole with baited breath."

The Last Solitary Morsel

It's a lonely life at the top of the world domination business: there are the do-gooders dressed in ridiculous combinations of spandex and lamé, corrupt cops looking for an easy cut, second-rate villains trying to steal your thunder, ordinary criminal enterprises elbowing into your territory, and, of course, there's the problem of henchmen: henchmen who are too dumb, too smart, too greedy, too flamboyant, too lazy, too treacherous, or too ambitious.

So how does a supervillain find good help? By dispensing with anything we might recognize as friendship and instilling fear into his professional relationships. As Machiavelli writes in *The Prince* (Chapter 27):

> Upon this a question arises: whether it be better to be loved than feared or feared than loved? It may be answered that one should wish to be both, but, because it is difficult to unite them in one person, is much safer to be feared than loved, when, of the two, either must be dispensed with.

3
Making the A-List

GALEN FORESMAN

> ***Advertisement:*** *Are you tired of driving the getaway car and cre-*
> *ating minor mischief around town? Duffle bags full of money not*
> *enough to warrant risking your life for a hopelessly deranged boss*
> *who fails to encourage and develop your inner strengths? Are you*
> *ready to start an independent life of running amuck and making*
> *a name for yourself? If so, then it sounds like you're ready to take*
> *the next steps in our patented Villainy Self-Improvement Classes,*
> *making benchmen and thugs like yourself into the supervillains*
> *you've always wished you could be.*

Step 1: Asking Questions and Getting Intimate
with Your Inner Evil

Young and old thugs alike come to us asking, "How can I be the
best supervillain I can be?" We find this question troubling for several reasons, but we can sum up our concerns like this: at its
essence this question is an expression of a deeply rooted confusion
in our core values as evil doers. There seems to us to be something
contradictory in wanting to be good at being bad when to be truly
bad we would need to be bad in every way possible. So the question isn't simply "*how* can I be the best supervillain?" but "can there
be a best supervillain?" Is there a best of the worst?

These questions are ultimately fundamental to who we are and
what we do as villains. They are things we should already know.
We hesitate to place too much blame on our hopelessly inadequate
and overtaxed public school systems, since many of us dropped

out or burned our schools to the ground (guilty). No, the real problem with many underlings these days is that they haven't spent enough time thinking about what it is for them *to be* villains. They're too busy being the nuts and bolts of truly villainous plots to understand the bigger picture of what makes those villainous plots so dastardly in the first place. In brief, they haven't taken the time to think about what makes a supervillain bad, and what it would take to make a supervillain the best of the worst.

At our core, we supervillains are deceptive. And so it's only natural that figuring out what it means to be the best of the worst would itself be a task full of deceit. This explains why there is something a little oxymoronic about how great supervillains can be. When people describe a supervillain as the worst, they are tricked and forced into saying that they are the best. But the same isn't true for descriptions of superheroes. When we describe a superhero as the worst, then there is no doubt that that superhero is the worst. The ordinary average person who describes a superhero as the worst means that that superhero is bad at what he does or, worse yet, they mean that that superhero does bad things. So how is it that describing supervillains as the worst and describing superheroes as the worst seems to mean two different things? Are supervillains so truly evil that they force the average person into a paradox of language by their very nature? We think so, and we think it is the key to unlocking some truly awesome villainy for ourselves!

(*Queue foreboding intro*)

In this step by step program we will help you unravel this mysteriously deceptive and central aspect to being a great supervillain. We will focus primarily on how we *evaluate* some of our paradigmatic supervillains, since words like "best" and "worst" are evaluative words. During this process we will draw upon the work of two great mad philosophical masterminds, Nelson Goodman and John Rawls, who devised a way of cheating when it comes to evaluation. Their work allows us to use a cheat-sheet for "discovering" those characteristics of our favorite supervillains that are both bad—in one sense of the word—and good at the same time. These characteristics are central to what it means to be a supervillain as opposed to a bad superhero. Our evaluations rely on a concept of supervillainy that is innately deceptive, and so a cheating is the only way to understand it. So here's your step by step cheaters guide for aiding up and coming villains who want to wield this evaluative paradox like a *true* supervillain.

Step 2: Who's Bad?

To solve the puzzle of what makes a supervillain bad and good at the same time, we must do what any card-carrying villain would do. We must cheat. Figuring out what makes a supervillain bad and good is a matter of evaluation. Evaluations are measurements of how good or bad we think something is, and so it should be pretty obvious that we evaluate things all of the time. More importantly for what we're doing here it's important to point out that when we make evaluations, we do so based on reasons. So, when we say, "Batman sucks," it's because we have reasons to think Batman sucks, like the fact that he keeps getting in the way of our awesome plans that totally would have worked swimmingly if it hadn't been for his pesky and overinflated sense of justice. But we digress.

Reasonable people remember the reasoning behind their evaluations and use that reasoning to form rules or guidelines for similar evaluations in the future. So if Batman sucks, and our reason for saying this is because he keeps getting in the way, then we could let that reason be a rule or guideline that helps us evaluate characters like Batman in the future. For instance, if Heroic Joe gets in the way of our awesome criminal activity, then our evaluation of him will be that he's sucky too. This is how reasonable people typically make evaluations.

However, we're not reasonable people, and if you really plan on becoming a supervillain, then you need to think about ditching all things reasonable too. Figuring out rules and guidelines is really boring, and since we're on our way to being great supervillains, we can't be expected to sit around thinking of insightful criteria for evaluation. That's for sissies and do-gooders. Batman might enjoy sitting around in the Batcave using his detective skills to determine evaluative criteria for great superheroes and evil supervillains so he can vet the Justice League roster or pick his next target on the most wanted lists, but we won't waste our time. As we said, we're going to cheat our way through this. Instead of determining criteria for evaluation first and then evaluating, we're going to do what any good cheater would do and get a list of the answers first.

We all know what's good and bad when we see it. We don't need any stinking evaluative criteria when we have our gut reactions. We didn't get to where we are today thanks to critically thinking through problems. No sir, and we certainly aren't starting now. Simply put, successfully stealing lots of money, that's good. Bossing people around, also good. Getting busted by a lowdown goody two shoes, that's bad. Being snitched on by some weasely nobody trying to curry favor with the D.A., that's very bad. So instead of thinking up various evaluative criteria to get a list of the best supervillains, we're going to skip right to the end and make up a list from gut reactions. Then we can then just make up reasons for why our list is that way. This brilliantly clever method for cheating your way through an evaluation was first used by the devilishly clever philosophical mastermind, Nelson Goodman, but was stolen—like any great supervillain would have it—given the name "Reflective Equilibrium," and popularized by John Rawls to support his theory of justice. Oh, the irony.[1]

So now that the method to our madness has been made clear, here's our response—in no particular order—to those infamous lyrics, "Who's Bad?"

1. **Apocalypse**

2. **Magneto**

3. **Lex Luthor**

4. **The Joker**

5. **Bizarro**

We know what you're thinking, "where's [insert your favorite villain here]?" Why didn't he or she make the list? Or, you might be thinking, "why the heck is that guy on the list?" Keep in mind that these are *our* evaluations and not yours. If you want to put someone else on your list, go ahead. The only important thing for this step is that your list have at least a handful of villains worthy of aspiration. If your list includes Asbestos Man, then you have issues that we probably can't help you with. Otherwise, we expect you'll have something workable. Evaluations that we make and endorse say something about who we are, and what we think is good and bad. So your list will say something about you, much like our list will say much about us. Of course, given the nature of our program maybe you should just steal our list from us.

---

[1] The irony is not that Rawls stole it from Goodman, because he didn't. I lied about that. The irony is that it's a cheater's way of defending a theory, especially one so lofty and arrogant as justice.

Step 3: Coming to Terms

Now that we have our lists, we can begin the process of figuring out why those villains on our lists are on those lists in the first place. Ultimately, your goal should be to get your name on these lists, and while threatening people may seem like a good start to getting yourself on these lists, it's only a start. Our lists reflect our evaluations of these villains, and we want others to evaluate us in the same way. Threatening someone may certainly affect their evaluation of you, but it is not the best method for achieving that goal. One of the primary differences between you and the truly awesome supervillains on our list is that you haven't come to terms with the difference between *your goals* and *your means* to achieving those goals.

The great supervillains on our list have big bad goals. Goals are the things that we want to achieve. They are sometimes called our "ends," because they are the final answer to questions about why we do the things we do. As villains, stealing money is something we do, but it isn't usually our ultimate goal or end. Stealing money is just a means to achieving those ends. If we were asked why we steal money, we might say that we need the money to corrupt the police force. Stealing money is a means to getting money that we can use to corrupt the police force. But corrupting the police force isn't even our ultimate goal; we corrupt the police force so that we can get away with doing things without worrying about the police trying to stop us. This means that corrupting the police force is yet another means to some end. So the question still remains, what is it that we *really* want to do?

Having power is an example of an end that many of us villains seem to have, but having power is like having money. School principals, crossing guards, and state legislatures have power, but it doesn't really make you all that evil, which villains need to be. A truly *super* villain does not shoot for such petty levels of power, but power, even absolute power, isn't all that great if there isn't something else you want to do. So if having power is your final goal, it's sort of an empty goal. Galactus, for example, didn't make our list of great supervillains for this very reason. He is one of the most powerful villains of all time, but the problem is that he's powerful like a hurricane or an earthquake is powerful. It's destruction without malice. Plus, an all powerful being might use all that power for good, because it isn't guaranteed that absolute power corrupts absolutely. Of course, our list of supervillains is mostly composed of very powerful individuals. Apocalypse, Bizarro, Magneto, and Lex Luthor are all very powerful in their own ways. But it isn't just their power that puts them on many lists of great supervillains. What they do with that power is really what makes them bad.

To transform yourself into a true supervillain, you need to get some goals that are big and bad. As we've already pointed out, getting power alone isn't always bad. You need power to reach your ultimate dastardly ends, but it won't be the power that puts you on a list of great supervillains. Oftentimes, it will be your other dastardly ends that do, like causing others to suffer for no other reason than it makes you laugh, like the Joker. If your only goal is to cause great suffering, then you'd be well on your way to becoming quite the villain. Generally speaking, if your goal is to cause great harm to many people, then you've got the right sort of goal for becoming a great supervillain.

Maybe a contrast with our hated rivals will help. A hero's ends are usually things like ensuring justice, peace, and freedom. In other words, a hero wants to help people. By contrast, a great supervillain needs to have goals that people do *not* think are good. Often when we describe a supervillain as one of the best of the worst, we are evaluating that villain based on his or her goals. What makes a supervillain great is that he or she does certain evil things, so the reason "best of the worst" seems contradictory is that we are making a positive evaluation of a villain based upon how positively we evaluate their *negative* goals.

There are, however, important exceptions to the goal oriented supervillain. Our lists of great supervillains are usually comprised of villains who cause great suffering on the way to achieving their goals. So in some cases a supervillain can be the best of the worst because of their *means* rather than ends. Magneto is very powerful, and having suffered at the hands of Nazis, he knows a thing or two about evil ends. His ends, on the other hand, aren't always so bad. In fact, in many ways they parallel the ends of the superhero, Charles Xavier, which is partly why he was able to lead the X-men for a time. In fact, often what separates a hero from a villain are the means employed to achieve their ends.

Reviewing our list of great supervillains in terms of their means and ends reveals much about the character of supervillains that aspiring hopefuls should emulate. The key to unlocking the villainous linguistic paradox of how to be the best of the worst depends on our ability to distinguish between *our evaluation of a supervillain's means or ends* and *our evaluation of the supervillain based on our evaluation of their means or ends*. To make it simple so your head doesn't hurt, we need to distinguish between evaluating a supervillain's actions and evaluating an evaluation of their actions. So, on the one hand we can say that a supervillain has big bad goals and goes about achieving them in big bad ways. On the other hand, after we have assessed that a supervillain has very evil goals and ways of achieving those goals, we might then evaluate that supervillain as the best at being bad. Since the *worst* of people are bad people, those that are the best at being bad must be the best of the worst.

Step 4: One Step Forward Means One Large Step Back

All this seems like the *right* way to do things, and if we're truly bad, then we can't be doing things the *right* way. Doing something the right way, as we've just laid it out, seems to fly in the face of all we've been teaching, and while we don't care much for consistency, we should at least leave you with one very important point to help you make sense of this final conundrum.

Take pride and joy in your failure. We cannot stress enough that your "success" in becoming a great supervillain depends in large part in *how* you go about achieving your goals, and not on whether you actually *achieve* those goals. Apocalypse has tried to dominate the human race several times, and while his devastation has always been great, he's always thwarted eventually. Lex Luther accomplishes many bad things, but his major evil goals are almost always foiled by that geek in blue and red. Magneto works tirelessly to secure mutant dominance, and yet, despite all his efforts, he's still working tirelessly. If these three supervillains were actually evaluated based on their successes, we'd find that they are for the most part colossal failures. So it isn't a huge leap in logic to conclude that part and parcel of being the best of the worst means failing big-time.

The Joker has probably the best understanding of this fine point. He goes to great lengths to make sure that he enjoys and takes pride in his wacky schemes. In fact, he seems to have ditched most lofty goals altogether and instead focused almost entirely on toying with his rival, bat-brains. If we think back to the original problem, to understanding what it means to being the best of the worst, we're reminded that an important difference between superheroes and supervillains is that when a normal person says that a superhero is great, we take it for granted that we know what that means. The superhero is great at what he or she does, and what he or she does is good things, like saving people. A superhero would not be great if they did not regularly succeed in their goals, even if they are lofty. The nice thing about being a supervillain is that we're in the exact opposite situation. Truly being the best of the worst is not about regularly succeeding in your goals, it's about failing to succeed. And we believe the evidence for this can be found in the fact that virtually every great supervillain has a superhero out to stop them. In fact, the more famous the superhero that's after you, the higher you normally rank as a baddie.

Step 5: The Last Laugh

Ironically, for many of you that was just good news. You're probably saying to yourself, "I'm just like [insert your favorite supervillain]! I always get busted." The truth is, you're nothing like your favorite supervillain. You're in a five-step program on how to be the best villain you can be. No self-respecting supervillain would have taken this course. Great supervillains make lists of great supervillains that have only *their* names on them. Remember, when you have big bad goals that you'll stop at nothing to achieve, you have to be self-centered.

So Step 5 is for you to give up, go home, or better yet take your frustration out on a friend. In fact, send them our way. We'll be happy to take them down a notch for you; that's what we do. After all, the Center for *Villainy Self-Improvement* didn't get to be experts on villains from reading a book. Finally, for those of you who still don't get it, we leave you with this parting encouragement from the great Greek wrestler/philosopher, Plato, "Ignorance is the root and the stem of every evil."

4

The Siren Song of Mad Science

KIRBY ARINDER and JOSEPH MILTON

EDITOR'S NOTE: *Although philosophical inquiry rarely poses risk to life and limb, its dangers to sanity are storied and quite real. It's therefore with some trepidation that we include the following contribution from Mr. Arinder and his possibly pseudonymous colleague "Milton." Their subject is an enquiry into the nature and principles of "mad science," and though we thought their project harmless, even useful, its contents have given us pause. The first and only draft of the essay was submitted in a strange and spidery hand, nearly illegible, with hastily scribbled notes in a second hand running throughout its margins. Though we considered omitting their work from this volume, Arinder appeared in person and insisted most strenuously that the essay be published. Not wishing to disturb his obviously fragile psyche, we assured him the essay would see print, and at this he subsided. However, since the book has gone to press, Arinder's sanity has failed altogether, and Milton is nowhere to be found. Thus, it is to our eternal regret that we did not halt their research before the terrible cost was paid. Here then is their essay as a testament and a warning to those who would land upon shores better seen from a distance, or plunge into stygian depths better sounded from above.*

The First Stirrings

We were once as you are now: half-formed, blind things, groping toward hidden truths whose extent we could not fathom. When we began our study of mad science—nay, *true knowledge* we should call it—we thought only to describe it, to capture and tame the concept with reason. What folly! Reason is bound by an infinite chain of oughts; the values of science are not tools but anchor weights. We have cast them off over the side and now bear truths beyond

31

sanity, yes, but also beyond good and evil. The wellspring of *mad science* is an idea as simple and as beautiful as the infinite dark of night, and it lurks within any scientific enterprise: *stop making value judgments when doing science.* With that simple idea the doors are thrown open, and vast realms of blameless power are yours!

Surely, you have said (for we hear your thoughts in our dreams) it cannot be that easy. Only a certain few have the talent and motivation necessary for ordinary science, and only a select few of these have it in them to surrender sanity. We admit, to glimpse the implacable mechanism by which our single principle produces every kind of mad science takes intellect and courage. But those willing to leave the timorous rabble behind will become the truly mad scientists they've always imagined they might be. Ask yourself, do you want to join this doubly elite group? Do you want to tap into the research funding that comes with world conquest? Do you want (finally!) to get revenge on those fools who laughed at you at the University? We know your answer already: *of course you do.*

Wait, we have revealed too much, too soon. How can we describe the thoughts that lead us inexorably to unlocking mad science, to the intoxicating power of unfettered genius? We will try to recall how the discovery was made when we were as you are now. All potential mad scientists know the positive qualities that mark the borders of madness: defying the natural order, crushing interlopers, and feeling that special pride the first time your abomination rises from the table. Everyone knows that's *what* mad scientists do, but the question is *how*? We sought out the *fundamental* difference between true mad science and its presumptuous imposters. Though mad science is an elite community, and suffers no imposters, nonetheless we met many, who were but moths before the true flame. Consider as a warning the sad spectacle of the following failures:

"I'm insane, and I do science!" said one poor fool who couldn't do science at all, much less the extra-difficult mad variety. Science is *hard*. If you try to do it while suffering from some sort of mental illness, you won't end up a Luthor, a von Doom, or a Frankenstein. You'll just end up an ordinary failure. Even if you can do science while being insane, the science you do will as often as not be of the ordinary sort: John Nash did his work on game theory while battling schizophrenia, but the Nash equilibrium only won him won him a Nobel Prize, it didn't run amok.

"Science helps me do evil!" said another misguided charlatan. Just about every evildoer in history has used science to serve his plans in one way or another, even if it was the science of flint-knapping, but that doesn't make them mad scientists. The mad scientist's guild is not so easy to join.

"I actually do science *evilly!*" said one promising acolyte. He at least tried to adopt an evil method, but bad isn't mad. It's perfectly possible to make evil part of scientific practice without being mad. After all, you can falsify grant proposals or perform gratuitous animal testing. Conversely, it's possible to do mad science without being evil if your inclinations don't run toward evil already.

Be warned: we unmasked these pretenders to true mad science, and learned that the mad scientist is no mere charlatan, quack, or Lysenkoist. At long last, we realized that the true mad scientist makes *madness* a part of scientific practice itself! The mad scientific revolution needs only a single approach to science to produces the benefits of insane enquiry. What is this approach, you ask? In the solitude of our study, we discovered that mad science is science unfettered by background theory or any of the guiding values that inform scientific practice.

Background theories describe how the world should be, and it is these that hold science back. Just imagine the logical, ethical, and metaphysical labor savings of casting aside background assumptions! After all, sane science is hard, layered with difficult, non-empirical theory about data selection, modes of inference, and hypothesis choice, and all that is *on top of* the difficult experimental work! Ignoring such fussy details lets you avoid the time and labor costs incurred by a more principled scientist, and you can get *right down* to the abhorrent human-animal hybrids! Of course, trying to do science without methodological values means doing the impossible, but if you can leave that problem to saner minds, then you too will have reached the boundaries of science's madness. When we crossed that threshold, our thoughts unbidden turned to strange benefits, and these we now share:

First, mad science is an attempt to perform an impossible action, and as such is paradigmatically mad. However, once freed from the bounds of consistency, imagine where your creativity can take you!

Second, in obscuring the role of the scientist's own values, it's almost impossible to talk meaningfully to practitioners of science who assume that science includes principles. You'll believe there is nothing more to be said once the data is in, and that means that any scientist who has the data and disagrees merits only one reply: "You MUST be wrong." This relieves you of the burden of communicating with your inferiors. After all, methodological values just obscure pure data, and hence they *must* be wrong. The data demands it, and for wasting your time they'll be lucky to avoid being fed to your quasi-human abominations!

Third, mad science enshrines the scientist's values as absolute by ignoring any objective or independent values that might exist contrary to the scientist's. In other words, you will always remain cold, cool, and intellectually objective, driven by data alone. As your self-modified abhuman brain extends its psychic tendrils throughout the world, you'll *know* this is not to gratify your own vast ego. Your work is valuable because science *proves* that the world is better that way.

Dark Victory

Already dazzled by the possibility that we were closing on the *secret* of mad science, we put aside our childish, lingering fear and began to investigate two of the great mad scientists whose methods we hoped to grasp. Both were men of prodigious intellect, both dared the boundaries of principle, and strangely—nay, tellingly!—both were named Victor.

The first is Victor Frankenstein! The mad scientist whose last name is practically synonymous with science run amok! He makes an excellent example because he's neither clinically insane nor evil. Instead, he selflessly helps plague victims, and the motive behind his monstrous deeds is to defeat death. He believes this will benefit humanity, but this just exhibits the mad scientist's confusion of imposed values with empirical data. Indeed, Frankenstein is defined by three central confusions of his own values with brute empirical fact. First, and most basic, Frankenstein's belief that life is purely a chemical process (especially prior to the discovery of DNA) is merely *compatible* with the empirical data about life, not *mandated* by it. His failure to see this as a value-stained hypothesis means he can only treat it as a fact about the world, discovered through his researches, and therefore empirically confirmed. Frankenstein doesn't just believe that life is chemical; he believes that he has *proven* that life is chemical, and objections are simply misguided, deluded, or irrational.

Frankenstein's willful confusion covers not only the theory that enables his grand quest, but the motivation for that quest and the methods by which he pursues it as well. The *Modern Prometheus* believes his research tells him not only that death is merely the cessation of chemical processes, but that death *should* be defeated, and by *any means* necessary. When others question this conclusion, they are ignoring evidence, not debating ethics. When he actually creates his artificial man, his creature's interests are utterly subordinated to his own. Frankenstein considers too late that there may be reasons not to dig up corpses or create a sapient being, only to later abandon it. As such, he is a paradigmatic case of mad science.

The other Victor is Dr. Doom. As a student, Victor von Doom's first major project was a machine with which he intended to rescue his mother from torment in the afterlife. Not only was this an affront to the natural order and the irrevocability of death, but a sure sign that Doom already had the scientific hubris that marks the best mad scientists. Not only was he after a huge, personally-motivated prize, but he ignored altogether the question of whether his machine ought to be built at all. Victor's roommate, Reed Richards, warned him that his afterlife-breaching machine would not work correctly, but Victor was far too *arrogant* to listen. It blew up on activation, and Victor was scarred by the experience. He swore vengeance on Richards after concluding that Richards had sabotaged his machine out of jealousy. Here again is mad science. Many theories could have explained the explosion: Reed Richards's theoretical worries might have been right, but so might Doom's conspiracy theory, or there may simply have been a roach in the machine. Why choose the conspiracy theory? Doom already hated his roommate, and so he leapt at the theory that discredited Richards. Of course, that's not how Victor saw it. For Doom, the data—the explosion, the scars, the crater where machine had been—could only be interpreted in one way. They admitted no other interpretation, so how could fail to choose the hypothesis that he did?

Troubled by his facial scars, Dr. Doom traveled to a remote monastery in Tibet, where he built a suit of powerful armor. To seal the deal, he had the faceplate of the armor placed onto his face while red-hot. Victor von Doom made *himself* his most terrifying project, a sort of grim reaper/robot, protected and cut off from the rest of humanity by his metal mask. This event in Doom's career offers physical manifestation of mad science in *action*: Mad science, science gone horribly wrong, is literally *dehumanizing* to the practitioner. Dr. Doom saw the genius in following where data *inevitably* leads, and the purity of a task as inexorable as the workings of his robotic decoys. Though they emulate his appearance outside, Doom's genius was to see the perfection of his creations' function within. *That* is the epitome of mad science! As we studied these men named Victor—who *were* victors—we realized that we were at the brink of understanding, at the edge of an unfathomable abyss. All that remained was to leap.

Inexorable Calculation

At this point we have let slip the simple secret of *how*: Moving from science to mad science depends upon rejecting the role of value in scientific methodology. Many of you might think this an easy demand to meet since you believe there is no role for value to play in science in the first place. You may think that proper science aims for objectivity, and isn't the absence of value judgments just what objectivity is? We congratulate this subset of readers for being so far gone. We were not so fortunate at the beginning, for we could not see how to avoid making value judgments in science. We were mired in principled sanity and saw no way out.

The design and implementation of experiments is often extraordinarily difficult. However, once designed, it's just a matter of pushing the right buttons on the mighty, pulsing-with-cosmic-power machine. Nature herself will tell us unambiguously if our theory was correct: either the portal to the Negative Zone opens or it doesn't. That's how we all learned it in that nursery of madness they call high school. The scientist formulates a theory, designs an experiment, tests the theory with the experiment, and rejects or confirms the theory. Even a robot lab assistant—or a Doombot—could carry out that kind of operation.

But the empirical data never picks out just one theory. The empirical data *underdetermines* theory choice. Any word that needs italics also needs an example, especially for those still shackled to their sanity, so imagine that a brilliant theorist posits that there is no one force called "gravity." Instead, there are two forces, the Power Cosmic and Anti-Life. The Power Cosmic attracts objects precisely twice as strongly as this foolish nonentity "gravity." Anti-Life, on the other hand, pushes objects away from one another in a manner equal and opposite to this hypothesized but silly gravitational force.

As such, the vector sum of the Power Cosmic and Anti-Life is always precisely identical in its effects to what we now call gravity.

You may find this alternative theory strange, but finding it scientifically illegitimate is another thing entirely. The theory makes predictions that are precisely as testable as our predictions from gravity. Any experiment which would tend to lend credence to the theory of gravity also lends precisely the same credence to the alternative theory. That's underdetermination. It's as though each experimental result gives us a dot—a "data point" you might say—and we have to draw the line that connects them with our theory. For any set of dots, there are an infinite number of lines you can draw. So it's not just the theory of gravity that's underdetermined in this way. For any theory, it's possible to produce alternative theories that are equally compatible with the empirical data, however late you stay up in the lab.

So how *do* scientists choose between the theory of gravity and the alternative? There are lots of *good* reasons to reject the Power Cosmic/Anti-Life theory. Maybe it's that the theory is unnecessarily complicated, or that it doesn't help us build useful technology, or that it's unwieldy to use. On the other hand, none of these criteria for tossing out one of the theories and keeping the other has anything to do with the data. Usefulness, simplicity, and convenience are methodological values we adopt because we *want* theories to be simple, useful, and convenient. What makes the theory of gravity better as a scientific theory relative to the alternative is that it fits better with our values, not the data.

Thanks to the problem of underdetermination, it is *impossible* to reach any conclusion based on empirical data without first establishing *some* methodological values that frame enquiry. Since these principles invoke *some* set of values, every example of scientific practice inevitably invokes the scientist's values. With that unpleasant task, every scientist is stuck. How then were we to cast off the restraints of value judgment, to let science proceed from the data alone? Finally we saw the answer: cheat. Choose without principles, and deny that your choices reflect any values whatsoever; there are only data, and data alone.

The Bottomless Well of Underdetermination

So how does embrace of a valueless approach to making scientific decisions get you all the benefits of mad science? How does this unlock everything from monstrous arrogance to making actual monsters? The principle cannot be met. It is impossible, and from the impossibility of acting only on data can the scientist who denies the role of his own methodological values impose them on everything. We had found the fertile contradiction that brought us into the heart of mad science! The blinding truth of it was simple: the mad scientist tries to remove methodological values from scientific enquiry. However, because scientific conclusions are in principle underdetermined by empirical data, the mad scientist draws her conclusions based on her avoidance of values, a goal she wishes her choices to affirm. Her conclusions *reveal* her values even as she denies them! So values are necessarily involved in producing any scientific knowledge, and that means mad scientists risk failure of an altogether different sort. What was *wrong* with Doom choosing to embrace the conspiracy theory in his fateful accident? That theory didn't contradict the available data. Nonetheless, there was something wrong with his *character*, and had he recognized and admitted to himself that he already hated Richards, he might have seen that he was attracted to a theory that licensed his hate. Instead he saw his choices as untainted, grounded solely on available data that permitted no other explanation.

By trying to do science without involving your values in the choice, you can develop the *hubris* that separates real mad scientists from their sane and lesser counterparts. We too were struck by the seeming paradox that denying one's own freedom leads to arrogance. However, if the data really did deny us the freedom to pick one theory over another, then we could not be blamed for embracing one theory over another. Without that liability, we can do whatever our inclinations tell us. In other words, trying act under no rule at all is really just acting under a rule to do whatever pops into your head! Denying the power to decide is a kind of hubris since you can't decide not to decide. Your will, the decision-making faculty, is divided against itself when it makes the attempt.

That's how mad science starts. By simply denying your own role in reaching scientific conclusions, you can get everything that makes mad science mad. From the denial of free choice in scientific activity comes the belief that science itself is immune to judgment, an activity without values. From this free pass springs the hubris that threatens established values, enforces irrational conformity, denies the importance of individual judgment, inappropriately privileges the scientist's perspective, and refuses to respect the object of scientific enquiry. Thus was the root of mad science laid bare! It was and is, above all else, the denial of the role of freedom in the world! As a seed it begins with the scientist's abnegation of responsibility, and ever greater it grows as all his projects proceed from the same self-centered values. At last, we had achieved it; we too had merged madness with science!

The Final Plunge

How will you bring madness to *your* science? Our time is short. Strange masters wait beyond the limits of rationality, and they call us hence, but let us lay a path of breadcrumbs for the foolish and unwary: cultivate the belief that your next experiment will solve the question you have before you once and for all, and that any price is worth paying for that knowledge. Avoid learning the history of science, and make a habit of justifying any method necessary for scientific progress. If someone is appalled at your laboratory practices on captured inferiors, tell yourself that opening new horizons of scientific knowledge is being clear-eyed, that your critics must be anti-science. Finally, and most importantly, if you can just embrace a scientific theory of how scientific values are chosen, then any role for your own values is sure to get lost as you march backward through the explanations. Yes, beyond the bounds of sanity are strange masters, and we can resist them no more! *Data, data beckons! We must follow, we will follow! None can resist, none can oppose—*

[Manuscript ends]

EDITOR'S POSTSCRIPT AND DISCLAIMER: *Though Arinder and Milton purported to offer the above work as original and complete, a manuscript discovered in the archives at a well-known New England university have revealed that their work in fact draws key passages from a much older manuscript fragment of uncertain origin. Obscuring matters further, handwriting analysis confirms that this essay's original draft was written in a hand matching that of the strange fragment. Though Arinder and Milton remain unavailable to enlighten matters, our present conjecture is that Arinder felt compelled not merely to lift selections from the strange manuscript, but to also preserve the strange geometry and oddly disturbing flourishes of its original written form.*

Phase Two

The Nature of Evil

5

V for Villain

ROBERT ARP

"I am the Devil, and I come to do the Devil's Work."

That's what V proclaims just before he kills Bishop Lilliman in the *V for Vendetta* series with an arsenic-laced communion wafer. Now Lilliman was an ex-storm trooper and a pedophile too, so he deserved to die anyway, right? Or did he? Remember V's proclamation above because it seems as if, almost automatically, people identify him as the hero of the story and have no problem with the fact that he kills people (albeit, evil and unjust people) in defense of his own version of the Gunpowder Plot.

V for Vendetta is set in an alternate post-nuclear-war world where the government of the United Kingdom is controlled by a George Orwellian *Nineteen Eighty-Four*-ish fascist party called Norsefire. Each area of the government represents parts of the "political body" with the Eye, the Ear, the Mouth, even the Finger controlling the totalitarian regime. V is a revolutionary living in the UK who dresses in a Guy Fawkes outfit and wants to destroy this government by bringing about a new, non-fascist government through anarchy. So, V begins killing government officials and blowing up buildings (like Guy Fawkes tried and failed to do in the famed Gunpowder Plot[1]), all while preaching anarchy in his own whimsical witty way with words. The long-term goal is that a more just society will emerge from the ashes of this anarchy.

---

[1] See Peter Brimacombe, *Guy Fawkes and the Gunpowder Plot* (Pitkin Unichrome, 2005).

ᴜw, on the face of it, we who come from democratic republics ᴌraise V's actions. After all, anything that reeks of Hitler-like fascism or Stalin-like communism (both are forms of totalitarianism) is evil, almost by definition, and someone challenging these regimes by killing, maiming, and blowing lots of stuff up seems to be heroically combating that evil. We praise the defender of democratic ideals as courageous, and we expect that defender to wreck havoc in these totalitarian regimes.

But is V really such a hero? His actions include (a) using people to further his own version of freedom as well as (b) disrespecting people in killing or harming them—even if they themselves are evil and act immorally. These actions can easily look like the deeds of a villain. After all, the series *is* called *V for Vendetta*, and a vendetta—understood as a murderous revenge or feuding—seems pretty darn immoral to me!

U for Utilitarian

Killing Bishop Lilliman probably saved dozens of children from being sexually abused, so someone might argue that this is a good thing. Heck, killing Hitler and Stalin likely would have saved millions, and almost anyone wishes they could rewind history and off the evil little bastards in their cribs! Followers of the famous philosopher, John Stuart Mill (1806–1873), argue that an action is morally good insofar as its consequences promote the most benefit, pay-off, or pleasure for the most persons affected by the decision. This view has been termed *utilitarian* because of the apparent usefulness (utility) to be found in generating the most satisfaction for the group of persons. The foundation of morality, as far as they're concerned, is simply happiness—actions are good insofar as they increase the pleasures or decrease the pains of people, in general.[2] "What is most beneficial for the most" is the utilitarian's slogan.

The utilitarian position justifies treating persons as means to the greater good of achieving benefit for the majority. For example, if the greater consequence of saving the group from some evil-doer requires killing one, two, or even a hundred people in the process,

---

[2] See Mill's *Utilitarianism*, or for a modern example Peter Singer's, *Practical Ethics* (Cambridge University Press, 1993).

then, on utilitarian grounds, this may be deemed morally correct. Again, think of the lives saved by offing Hitler or Stalin.

Or, if you're with a group of people on a lifeboat trapped at sea, you might be justified in taking the rations from the guy who is near death or beyond help; you could even be justified in killing one person and surviving on that person's flesh until you're saved by a passing ocean liner! It's the whole "killing one to save many" kind of thinking. Back in 1972, a Uruguayan soccer team crashed in the Andes mountains and survivors actually had to eat the dead.[3]

Also, killing that pedophile Lilliman prevented a lot of potential suffering in the *V for Vendetta* universe just as locking up pedophiles (or killing them, if it happens) eases a lot of minds in our universe. Mr. Spock said it best in *Star Trek II: The Wrath of Khan*, and he even walked the walk by sacrificing his own life: "the needs of the many outweigh the needs of the few . . . or the one."

Straightforward examples of this utilitarian position can be found in the actions of members of the Norsefire, who think nothing of using the members of society to promote the so-called good of the society as a whole. Adam Susan and the rest of the "political body" think that the "end" of a peaceful, unified state justifies the "means" of torturing, terrorizing, or killing any of its citizens. In fact, people are treated like mere objects in the alternate UK, which strikes us as downright wrong (and strange) because it's normally the other way around; people use objects like cars, computers, and can openers to get what they want, achieve goals, or gain satisfaction.

Bishop Lilliman is an obvious user of people for his own pleasures; but consider Helen Heyer, the wife of Conrad Heyer (who is in charge of the Eye, the United Kingdom's closed-circuit TV system). She is described as a ruthless bitch who uses people to gain information, power, trust, or sexual pleasure—even her own husband. Such behavior strikes us as wrong because we think of people as conscious beings, worthy of dignity and respect, who never should be treated like mere objects, for self *or* group benefit.

S for Similar

Characters in *V for Vendetta* constantly are portrayed as having instrumental value, to be used like mere things. We have already

---

[3] Read about this story, and others, in Frank Spalding, *Plane Crash: True Stories of Survival* (Rosen, 2007).

mentioned Bishop Lilliman, Adam Susan, and Helen Heyer as people who treat others as instruments, whether it be for power, pleasure, political gain, or peace. And someone might argue from the utilitarian perspective that Susan is the most moral of the three because he at least uses people as a means to some greater good, whereas Lilliman and Heyer are just plain selfish users of people for their own satisfaction.

However, V himself can be considered as a user of people for "greater purposes" as well as his own purposes. Like Susan, V also acts like a utilitarian when he systematically kills the major officials of Norsefire for the greater good of bringing about an anarchy from which—he hopes—a more just governing body will emerge. V also allows himself to be used as an instrument of freedom. His very life as the Guy Fawkes savior of the United Kingdom, and his death so that Evey and others may "carry the torch" both indicate that he intends to sacrifice himself for the greater good of the society in which he resides. So, for V the end of anarchy-to-justice justifies the means of killing Norsefire members as well as sacrificing himself . . . a bit like Mr. Spock.

Consider the time when V breaks into Jordan Tower to broadcast an anarchist speech and captures Roger Dascombe, dressing him up in his own mask and costume so as to escape. Dascombe is killed by his own storm troopers when they enter the room and mistakenly think that it's V they're killing. Of course, V knew better, and we are left with a "serves that bastard right" kind of taste in our mouths.

Further, think of the time when V dupes Evey Hammond into believing that she has been captured by the Fingermen, which includes her torture and interrogation (believe it or not!). Eventually, V reveals the hoax and tells her that he did this for Evey's own good, so that she may "know" her own identity and freedom. Evey agrees—(surprisingly—and considers what V did for her as something positive and necessary for her own well-being. I don't know about you, but I would verily have kicked V in the vitals if he did that to me!

I question whether V is morally justified in any of his utilitarian actions. In the case of Dascombe, it's true that Dascombe is an evil jerk; but that's beside the point. The point is that V clearly used another human being as a shield or other object of *deflection*. In Evey's case, the objectification apparently leads to something good, but that's beside the point as well. V clearly used another human being, this time as a mirror or object of *reflection*. After all, V tells Evey that he wanted her to experience what he went through. Thus, the question arises as to whether V's vicious behavior is villainous and should be vilified rather than validated and venerated (couldn't resist, at least once in this chapter . . . Okay, twice if you count the "verily V in the vitals" comment). Either as an object of deflection (a good thing) or object of reflection (another good thing), these people *still* were used as objects, and they should not have been.

It should be clear that I am claiming that *both* V *and* Norsefire act like utilitarians: they both view people as means, even to the extent that they can potentially be killed for some greater good. Now, you might say to me that the "greater good" in both of these cases is different. The greater good for Norsefire is really an evil empire of totalitarian injustices, so what they're doing is evil and they should be stopped. Thus, on utilitarian grounds, V's killing of them is justified. On the other hand, the greater good for V is ultimately freedom for all from this oppressive political regime (or, in Evey's case, freedom from an enslaving part of herself). Thus again, on utilitarian grounds, V's killing of Norsefire is justified. There is obviously something to this kind of objection; however, my point is that there is something wrong with using a person as a means, period, whether it be for your own good or some greater good.

K for Kantianism

Should we ever use another person as a means for any reason, even if by using that person lives will be saved on a lifeboat, in the Andes, or in the UK? Our first instinct might be to say "hell, yes!" If some friggin' terrorist has a bomb that will kill thirty people, or even one other person, and we could prevent the killing by wasting that terrorist, who in their right mind would *not* waste him? Believe it or not, however, it is possible to argue that killing one to save many, in certain situations, is immoral. To see how and why, we need to be introduced to the famous philosopher, Immanuel Kant (1724–1804).

Kant observes that persons are unique in that they are conscious, rational beings, capable of making their own free and informed decisions. From the fact that humans are unique in this way, Kant tells us that we should "act in such a way that you always treat humanity, whether in your own person or in the person of another, never simply as a means, but always at the same time as an end." Kant is not ruling out the moral possibility of treating people as means. After all, we have to use people for goods, services, information, and such things in order to live our daily lives. What he is ruling out is treating a person as *nothing but a means* for such ends. In other words, a person must always be treated as an end in him or herself even while also being used as a means to some other end. Because we are conscious, rational beings, persons have a "sanctified" *intrinsic* value (as ends) and not just an *instrumental* value (as a means to an end) like some object, tool, thing, or instrument.

For Kant, morally right decisions are those that treat a person as an end, and morally wrong decisions are those that treat a person as a mere instrument or means to an end.[4] Also, Kant makes it clear that any kind of murder is considered immoral since the one murdered is being used by the murderer for the sake of the murderer's satisfaction, malice, or other selfish reason. Interestingly enough, the same goes for the avenger, like V, where a person is used for the sake of vengeance.[5]

So for Kant, that people's have conscious rational capacities means they are free and autonomous beings with an inalienable worth or dignity. Because of this intrinsic worth, a person should *never* be treated as a mere object, whether that person is a prince or pauper, saint or son of a bitch. It's primarily from this Kantian perspective that we are disgusted by Helen Heyer's actions, as she continually manipulates her husband Conrad (mostly with sex), while furthering her goal of controlling the country from behind the scenes once he gains power. But maybe we should also be disgusted by V's actions, too.

I for I Want to be a Whore, So U for Use Me

But hang on a second. It's my body, and I'll do what I want to do with it, damn it! What if, as a fully rational being who is self-ruling

---

[4] See Immanuel Kant, *Foundations of the Metaphysics of Morals* (Prentice Hall, 1989). A classic exposition of Kant's moral philosophy can be found in Onora O'Neill, *Constructions of Reason: Explorations of Kant's Practical Philosophy* (Cambridge University Press, 1990).

[5] *Foundations of the Metaphysics of Morals*; also Suzanne Uniacke, "Why Is Revenge Wrong?" *Journal of Value Inquiry* 34 (2000), pp. 61–69.

and autonomous, I *want* to be used? The word *autonomy* comes from two Greek words meaning self (*auto*) and law (*nomos*), highlighting the facts that a rational person is "self-ruling" and his or her own informed decisions should be respected. What if I take it upon myself to assume all the risks of being used in a situation? The idea here is that if a fully rational person chooses to engage in some action—as long as the action doesn't harm anyone else—then that person is fully justified in making that decision, even if the decision puts that person in the position of being used by another person or group of persons. Since a person's innate dignity and worth are tied to rational autonomy, what is most significant in making a moral decision is whether a person's *freedom in rationally informed decision-making* has been respected.[6]

Think of fully rational adults joining the army with the knowledge that they may be sacrificed for the sake of the nation in time of war. Or, think of persons getting hired at a huge corporation knowing full well that the ultimate goal of the company is to make money, and that they may lose their jobs in a down-sizing that would keep the corporation afloat. For that matter, there would be nothing immoral about one V-aligned spy using another Fingermen-aligned spy as a sexual conduit for information, since both spies freely and autonomously have agreed to engage in these behaviors knowing full well that they are using and being used. A woman might knowingly and willingly sign up to be a member of the Fingermen (the secret police in *V for Vendetta*), fully aware of the fact that there is a bigger totalitarian plan in the country, and that she is expendable in light of this bigger plan. In other words, a member of the Fingermen makes a fully conscious choice to be just another "cog in the wheel" and she seems fully morally justified in doing so.

Isn't it the case that I'm being treated like an object if I am not allowed to make my own decisions? In other words, *I am being treated like an object in not being allowed to be treated like an object!*

This seems to set up a conflict in moral decision-making process between, on the one hand, the idea that one should never use

---

[6] See Thomas Hill, *Auonomy and Self Respect* (Cambridge University Press, 1991); Christine Korsgaard, *The Sources of Normativity* (Cambridge University Press, 1996); Timothy Madigan, "The Discarded Lemon: Kany, Prostitution, and Respect for Persons," *Philosophy Now* 21 (1998), pp. 14–16.

another person as an instrument, and on the other hand, the idea that fully rational persons have the freedom to make their own well-informed decisions, even if those decisions include using or being used by another person. In fact, there is one camp of "moral sanctity" Kantians who would argue that it's immoral to objectify a person, no matter what.[7] And there is another camp of "moral autonomy" Kantians who would argue that, as long as all parties are fully aware of the parameters, risks, and consequences of the situation, nothing immoral occurs in the whole using/being used process. These same thinkers often argue that to deny a person the freedom to choose to be of use to someone else would itself be immoral because such a denial violates a person's autonomy as a rational, wholly free decision-maker. To deny a person the freedom to choose is to reduce that person to an object, since, after all, mere objects lack choices.[8] Here, we have a bit of a stand-off. From the moral *sanctity* perspective, objectification is morally wrong (and even V might be the villain, here); from the moral *autonomy* perspective, objectification can be morally right.

B for Back to Utilitarianism

We often make decisions based upon the best consequences for all of the people involved. If consequences are the key to determining whether objectification is morally wrong, then we can see that treating persons as objects has negative ramifications and, hence, is morally unacceptable. Think of all of the instances of slavery throughout human history and all of the negative consequences that follow. Or, think instances of totalitarian regimes—like Stalin's Soviet Union, Hitler's Third Reich, or the Norsefire in *V for Vendetta*—where persons were tormented, tortured, unjustly treated, displaced from their homes, and murdered all for the greater "good" of some state or ideology. Further, consider the con-

---

[7] Andrea Dworkin, *Pornography: Men Possessing Women* (Perigee, 1981); Catherine MacKinnon, *Feminism Unmodified: Discourses on Life and Law* (Harvard University Press, 1988).

[8] Ann Garry, "Pornography and Respect for Women," in John Arthur, ed., *Morality and Moral Controversies* (Prentice-Hall, 1993), pp. 395–421: Timothy Madigan, " The Discarded Lemon," pp. 14–16; Sibyl Schwarzenbach, "On Owning the Body," in James Elias, Vern Bullough, Veronica Elias, and Gwen Brewer, eds., *Prostitution: On Whores, Hustlers, and Johns* (Prometheus, 1998), pp. 345–351.

sequences to our communities of treating women or men like sex objects, as is common in advertising, television shows, and movies. Such objectification has been linked to violence against women, date-rape, eating disorders, and a general disrespect for the sanctity of intimate relationships.[9]

However, as crazy as it may seem at first, it's possible to argue that objectification sometimes has had—and does have—good consequences. Hence, on utilitarian grounds, one can argue that forms of objectification are moral and should be promoted. One could maintain that the objectification of persons, as when V does so, has good consequences for the community.[10] In fact, we almost without thinking cast V as the hero because we believe that his terrorist-type of actions are all for the ultimate good.

That said, we should at least recall the Kantian sanctity position that a person should never be used, and in that light we should at least re-think V's heroic image.

There is more to this. Important virtues include honesty, courage, prudence, generosity, integrity, affability, and respect, to name just a few. Respect is the key virtue for our purposes here. The person who has cultivated respect for persons in his or her character naturally will not objectify another person. When one treats a person as an object, one empties another of their intrinsic dignity, value, and worth, affecting both the one doing the objectifying and the one being objectified. In effect, the problem lies in the psychological ill-effects of treating another as less than a person.[11]

---

[9] See the resources, videos, and articles at www.vawnet.org; also, Lisa Tessman, "Critical Virtue Ethics: Understanding Oppression as Morally Damaging," in Peggy DesAutels and Joanne Waugh, eds., *Feminists Doing Ethics* (Rowman and Littlefield, 2001), pp. 79–99; Kathleen Barry, *The Prostitution of Sexuality* (New York University Press, 1995); Susan Dwyer, *The Problems of Pornography* (Wadsworth, 1995).

[10] For utilitarian arguments defending objectification, see Sarah Bromberg, "Feminist Issues in Prostitution," in *Prostitution: On Whores, Hustlers, and Johns*, pp. 294–321; Marti Hohmann, "Prostitution and Sex-Positive Feminism, in *Prostitution: On Whores, Hustlers*, pp. 322–331.

[11] See Elizabeth Brake, "Sexual Objectification and Kantian Ethics," in *Proceedings and Addresses of the American Philosophical Association* 76 (2003), pp. 120–131; Lisa Tessman, "Critical Virtue Ethics: Understanding Oppression as Morally Damaging;" Barbara Andrew, "Angels, Rubbish Collectors. and Pursuers of Erotic Joy: The Image of Ethical Women," in *Feminists Doing Ethics*, pp. 119–134; Marilyn Friedman, *What Are Friends For? Feminist Perspectives on Personal Relationships and Moral Theory* (Cornell University Press, 1993).

So the Kantian argument weighs against V's actions, but we might be able to mount a utilitarian case against V as well. We must ask what will ultimately be best for a community as a whole:

1. As a fully rational and autonomous person, should I treat myself or another fully rational and autonomous person as a means, rather than as end in him or herself?

2. What kinds of consequences will result for other persons affected by my action and me if I do decide to treat myself or another fully rational and autonomous person as a mere means, rather than as an end in him or herself?

3. Do I want to foster a virtue in myself, my kids, my family, my community, or in my world whereby others are seen as persons *worthy of respect*, fundamentally equal to myself, making it such that one person is not permitted to objectify another person?

4. Do I want to foster a virtue in myself, my kids, my family, my community, and/or in my world whereby certain others are seen as emptied of the intrinsic dignity, value, and worth?

Of course, these questions are "loaded" to a great extent; but this is done to make a point. So, think of the various *V for Vendetta* personalities, including V himself. It seems that, if 1. and 2. do not halt us in our tracks and stop us from objectifying ourselves or one another, then 3. and 4. give us pause to consider what kind of person we would becoming if we continually objectify other people.

Kant has a famous line where he says that you can teach a nation of devils to set up a society and be moral. Here, Kant is pointing out that acting according to principles—especially a respect for someone else's autonomy—is what is moral, no matter what kind of person you are.[9] From the Kantian moral sanctity perspective, V may be right, then, that he is the devil come to do the devil's work of using people, which disrespects them and, in itself, is therefore evil.

[12] Immanauel Kant, *Perpetual Peace* (London: FQ Publishers, 2007).

6

What Magneto Cannot Choose

JARED POON

Magneto, our favorite master of magnetism, is walking down one of the hallways of his stronghold in the Savage Land, on his way to a poetry recital by his daughter the Scarlet Witch. He passes his benevolent gaze over the mutant children that throng the place, precocious and carefree.

Suddenly, alarms wail—the Sentinels have found his mutant utopia and are attacking *en masse!* Beams of energy crash through glittering domes and tall spires as the Sentinels hunt down the mutant residents. Magneto is furious! Rising high into the air on eddies of magnetic force, he bends his will toward the attacking robots and reels them in, exerting his mutant mastery over magnetism to rewire their neural circuits. The Sentinels, now reprogrammed to terminate regular humans rather than mutants, fly off towards New York City, Magneto himself leading from the front. "You have my word, my brothers," he promises his subjects, ". . . a thousand—no, a hundred thousand—human beings will die tonight for every mutant lying bleeding at your feet." (All this is as recounted in *Ultimate X-Men #05*.)

Magneto means to kill every human man, woman, and child in the United States of America, and that is a monstrous act, right? At first glance, the moral metaphysics of the world of comics is about as sophisticated as the primary-colored spandex (or unstable molecular) costumes of the superheroes and supervillains that inhabit it. There are good guys and bad guys. The good guys are dashing and beautiful, and fight for what most of us regard as noble and good. They are people like Charles Xavier, who preaches harmony between humans and mutants, Spiderman who fights crime because such great responsibility comes with great power, and Superman, the moral paragon who stands for truth, justice, and the American way.

The bad guys are people like Magneto, cruel and evil, often bent on either destruction or world domination. Not only are they usually not as pretty as their heroic counterparts (consider how many supervillains are outwardly scarred—the Joker, Victor von Doom, Weapon-X's Colonel Wraith, just to name a few), their maniacal laughs, tendency to monologue at crucial moments, and callous disregard for life makes it hard to think of them as credible evildoers, that is, as *anything but* two-dimensional supervillains.

Take a moment, however, to step behind the eyes (and mask) of a supervillain—say, Mister Mxyzptlk, or Moses Magnum, or Magneto himself. Does a supervillain see himself as a supervillain? Does he see his own actions as evil? I believe the answer to both of these questions is *no*. Supervillains, from the vile Annihilus to the time-travelling Professor Zoom, see themselves as acting not for the sake of evil, but for the sake of the good. That is, supervillains *always* direct their actions at what is good: the monster never sees a monster in the mirror.

I can hear the grunts of outrage even from here. But don't commit me to Arkham Asylum just yet—even a poor philosopher deserves a fair hearing.

The Choices of the Master of Magnetism

Just as every superhero or supervillain worth his salt requires an origin story, our discussion about how supervillains see themselves will be well-served by a brief examination of the historical background. For that, let us return to the thirteenth century, where our key figures reside. On the one side, we have the *intellectualists* (we'll see what they're all about shortly), fronted by St. Thomas Aquinas. Thomas famously dictated several different texts to several different secretaries at the same time—not that flashy as a superpower, but still useful. Arrayed against the intellectualists, we have the *voluntarists* with their poster-boy, William of Ockham. William is, of course, the very razor-wielding individual who reminds us not to multiply entities beyond necessity, something Jamie Madrox would do well to remember.

The disagreement between the intellectualists and the voluntarists was about the nature of *choice*. Both sides agreed on the general picture of how choices are made—there are three steps. The *senses* first gather information from the surroundings. This information is sent to the *intellect*, which looks at the various options and judges which one is better. The judgment of the intellect is then presented to the *will*, which chooses. Here's how this might work in Magneto's case.

Recall Magneto, hovering over his island sanctuary in the Savage Land, ready to depart and wreak havoc on the human race. How does he come to make that choice? The senses are first engaged—Magneto *sees* the giant robots of purple and chrome, he *hears* the cry of injured mutants, he *smells* the acrid mixture of blood and fire. This sensory information is presented to the intellect, which sorts through them, lays out several courses of action, and judges which are better and which are worse. For the sake of simplicity, let us say that there are three options, as determined by the intellect:

1. **Help the Sentinels burn everything to the ground.**

2. **Destroy the Sentinels in the skies over the Savage Land.**

3. **Reprogram the Sentinels to hunt humans instead of mutants, and send them back at New York.**

The work of the intellect is not done. Not only is it in charge of figuring out what the options are, it is in charge of figuring out which one is best. Magneto's intellect would find options 1. and 2. less than satisfactory, so option 3. it is! The options are all presented to the will, along with which one has been judged to be the best. The will then chooses, or moves the person to act, which in this case means that Magneto sets off to New York to kill several million people. It's worth taking a moment to make sure the terms and concepts remain clear. Ordinarily, when people talk about choosing something, they mean they're just making up their mind. However, on the three step model above, making up one's mind is not choosing, but making an intellectual judgment. For both Thomas Aquinas and William of Ockham, choosing means the will engages you to *act*.

But just what the will can choose is where the intellectualists and voluntarists part ways. For Thomas and his intellectualist friends, the will *must* choose what the intellect presents as being better. If Magneto's intellect judges that the protecting his people and taking revenge on his enemies is the best option, his will cannot choose otherwise, and on that basis he *will* then act. On the other hand, for Ockham and his voluntarist buddies, the will is free to choose even the option that is presented as worse. If the voluntarists are right, then Magneto could choose to destroy the Sentinels in the skies over the Savage Land, or help the Sentinels burn everything to the ground, even if these were judged to be in every way worse than another option.

Common sense might side with the voluntarists at first glance. After all, it's surely *possible* for Magneto to have stopped at merely destroying the Sentinels, no matter what judgments his intellect might have produced. But this intuition deserves careful examination—just what *is* going on when we do the things we do?

His Judgments Revealed

The things we do come in at least two flavors. There are things we do intentionally, and things we do unintentionally. In the first category are actions we *choose* to do: discussing the latest Batman movie or cutting the green wire to defuse the gamma bomb. In the second category are things like sneezing, or absent-mindedly scratching an itch, or falling over when shoved. Only the actions that belong in the first category seem morally interesting. After all, if Superman sneezes and incidentally puts out a fire, we don't consider him a virtuous person just for that, nor do we consider the sneezing a morally praiseworthy action. Since we are concerned with good and evil here, let us focus on the kinds of actions that are intentional.

These kinds of actions have a peculiar structure—one might think of them as *acts for ends*. That is, there are at least two components to the action—the thing we do, and why we do it. What it is that we do is often the outwardly observable part of the action. When Magneto exerts his formidable control over magnetic fields to stop a jet from crashing to the ground, that is certainly an awe-inspiring act, but we don't understand the action fully until we know *why* he did it. In other words, we look for *reasons* for his doing what he did. Was it compassion that moved him, or was it a mere arrogant display of power? The *reasons* behind the act are called *ends*, and they matter to our understanding and evaluation of people's choices.

If this is right, then we need more information to have a complete story about Magneto's choice to give the Sentinels a new directive to seek and kill humans. We need to know not just Magneto's options (and their corresponding acts), but the ends those the acts would serve. Only then can we really understand how Magneto's intellect weighs the options against one another and comes to a judgment.

Consider option 1., that Magneto helps the Sentinels burn everything to the ground. It's certainly *possible* that this is an option that serves *one* of Magneto's ends. He might want to spite his son Quicksilver, or he might think that burning it all to the ground would help get rid of the Savage Land's mosquito problem. Compare this with option 3., that Magneto neutralizes the Sentinels' attack and reprograms them for revenge. This might serve another of Magneto's desired ends, namely, to protect his people and build a world where they can live without fear or ostracism. Coming to the judgment about which of those two options is best involves some sort of weighing. Is protecting his fellow mutants a more desirable end than getting rid of the mosquitoes? Magneto has to give up one to pick the other, and so it is necessary to figure out which end is more important. Not surprisingly, he chooses to help his subjects.

Our question was, can Magneto choose to help the Sentinels burn down his stronghold, even if doing so appears *in no way* the better option? Now we can be more precise about what we're asking. Can Magneto act contrary to his own best judgment that there are no better ends, or combinations of ends, than are served by reprogramming the Sentinels as vengeance weapons against humanity?

It would not just be strange for Magneto to make a choice like this in the scenario we have described, but impossible if it's also true that making choices requires voluntary action. We observed earlier that voluntary choices (the kind open to moral assessment) require intentions. If Magneto has no prior intention behind his action, then reprogramming the Sentinels can be no more than a spastic flailing of limbs and a haphazard release of magnetic power. But if intentions pick out the reasons *why* we act in any case when we do, then because reasons are the province of the intellect, intentions actually *reveal* the intellect's judgments.

Maybe you don't find this compelling so far. Perhaps you have the intuition that Magneto *could* of course choose to help the Sentinels burn everything to the ground. The above account does not deny this possibility. What is denied is that this can be *chosen*—acted upon—if Magneto's intellect judges that this is not the best option. For Magneto to choose otherwise means that his intellect sees reasons to choose this option that outweigh whatever reasons there are to choose the alternative. These might be the aforementioned pique at Quicksilver, or annoyance at mosquitoes, or perhaps as part of a grand plan to lull Professor Xavier into complacence. Without reasons of this sort that make this option better than the others, all things considered, Magneto cannot choose it. Ockham and the voluntarists are wrong, and Aquinas and the intellectualists are right—the will cannot choose against the judgment of the intellect.

Beyond the World's Ends

So we've established that even the superior genes of Magneto cannot let him escape the requirement that the will choose what the intellect judges best. Is that all the work that the intellect does? The ends of actions are the reasons why one performs those actions. Magneto's ends in exerting his magnetic powers was to immobilize the Sentinels, but some ends can be subordinate to others. Magneto's reasons for wanting to immobilize the Sentinels might be to keep his mutant brethren safe, but this might in turn be subordinate to further ends. Magneto's reason for protecting his people is that he thinks the world is better if they are safe than if they are not. That's a new end, and his decision to reprogram the Sentinels advances it. That one option is *better* than another is, we usually think, sufficient reason for us to do something.

But there's a further thought here. An option's being better means that it's good relative to the alternatives, and if we could line up every option we might have, then in principle we might be able to identify *ultimate* reasons or ends, and this is what the intellectualists identified as the source of *moral* good. So our actions are ultimately guided by our view of the good, and this is true not just for Magneto, but for supervillains, superheroes, and everyone else as well. This is especially clear when we think about the motivations and ends of some of the most compelling supervillains. Magneto wants to build a world where his fellow mutants can live free of fear. Ra's al Ghul wants to cleanse the Earth and return it to a pristine state. Apocalypse wants to help mutants evolve. All of these goals are, as they stand, laudable.

Even the motivations that appear selfish or petty are directed at what appears to them to be the good. Lex Luthor's thirst for vengeance against Superman is his way of setting right the cosmic scales—after all, where would humanity be if it wasn't always looking beyond its own resources for salvation from an *alien*. Even in these cases, the actions of these supervillains are directed at what appears to them to be the good, though all the rest of the world disagrees. Magneto's fatherly advice to Cyclops is quite revealing:

> "I know it's hard, Scott. But you've got to stand back and look at the bigger picture. Even the best of us must do abhorrent things *in the pursuit of the greater good* sometimes . . . [Humans are] a fundamentally flawed creation and it's our *duty* to replace them at the earliest opportunity. As the more intelligent species, one might even say that it's our *moral responsibility*." (*Ultimate X-Men #05*, emphasis mine)

Mutants, Madmen, and Monsters

Wait, you might protest, surely it cannot be the case that every supervillain sees himself as doing what is good. How do we then account for supervillain-groups such as "The Brotherhood of Evil Mutants"? Doesn't the name suggest that they understand themselves to be evil?

The name "The Brotherhood of Evil Mutants" first appears as a newspaper headline in *Strange Tales*, Volume 1, #120, and it could well be where the members of the Brotherhood got the name. Furthermore, both Mystique and Toad have noted that the name is meant to be ironic, at once showing both the group's awareness of the general public's disapproval of them and their disregard for public disapproval. Their appropriation of the name from the newspaper headline could easily be understood as the equivalent of a rude gesture to the world—"So you think all mutants are evil? Well, here we are—your 'evil' mutants."

Consider similar cases in the real world. Like the persecuted mutants of Marvel's universe, many real-world persecuted groups have carried out similar appropriations, transforming erstwhile insults into badges of honor, deliberately stripping slurs of their negative connotations by flaunting them (as they flaunt their own stigmatized identities in open, cheerful defiance of their persecutors). Slurs directed at ethnic groups, sexual identities, and even people from certain states (such as "Yankees") have been willfully adopted by the groups themselves. Likewise, it is far from implausible that a group of ostracized mutants might take upon themselves the label they have been saddled with, and wear proudly the title of "evil." The idea we have been looking at, that all supervillains see themselves as aiming for the good—even if they disagree with other people about what that ultimately is—is compatible with the presence of groups such as the Brotherhood of Evil Mutants, the Masters of Evil, and the Injustice League.

There is a further wrinkle presented by some supervillains whose actions are incomprehensible. Mephisto and Etrigan are demons, incarnations of the concept of evil. Bizarro seems to desire the opposite of what one would normally desire, and so sometimes aims for evil instead of the good. We have in the same category characters like Hunger, or Death, whose very natures compel them to act in a certain way. As such, the decision procedures of these characters are nothing like our own—they are truly alien, and any attempt at understanding their motivations and psychological structures is doomed to be no more than mere approximation.

However, barring the incomprehensibly alien, morally credible supervillains act only for the good as it appears to them. If this is right, then any moral censure we direct at them will have to be carefully aimed. Supervillains are supervillains not because they want to do evil, but because they have a deeply flawed conception of the good.

7
Bright Colors, Dark Times

CHRISTOPHER ROBICHAUD

Time was when superheroes and supervillains stood out as clearly and as brightly as the primary-colored costumes they wore, making decisions against a moral background painted starkly in black and white.

This was the Silver Age of Comics, with its righteous superheroes, its diabolical supervillains, and nothing in between. The major comic book publishers each had their respective moral paragons at both ends of the spectrum. Superman and Captain America defended the values of truth, justice, and the American way. They waged a tireless campaign against the likes of Lex Luthor, with his insatiable quest for power, and the Red Skull, with his relentless Aryan fascism. Good was spelled with a capital 'G', Evil with it a capital 'E', and that was that.

But no more. In the Modern Age of Comics (sometimes called the Iron Age), gray has been added to the palette that colors the moral universe. The hero in *V for Vendetta* commits acts of terrorism. Batman's aggressive pursuit of criminals clearly violates some of their rights. And Magneto's violent campaign against the government is motivated in part by the government's attempt to eradicate mutants. These actions are no longer obviously right or wrong. And the paragons of good and evil themselves? Superman and Captain America are now frequently caricatured as one dimensional boy scouts, and the most compelling supervillains exhibit a moral complexity more consistent with anti-heroes than cackling arch-fiends.

So the lines that once clearly separated good from evil have apparently dissolved. Stories like *Red Son*, and *Lex Luthor: Man of*

Steel (among many others) attempt to fill the space between these moral endpoints with many shades of gray. But more than that, they also challenge the idea that there are any straightforward distinctions between the opposite ends of the moral spectrum, suggesting instead that the moral differences between Captain America and the Red Skull, or between Superman and Lex Luthor, are ultimately a product of place and time, of perspective, rather than of some underlying absolute moral truths.

In this respect, today's comics capture today's sensibility about morality. For many people, the idea that there are absolute moral facts has given way either to a kind of moral relativism or to a kind of moral nihilism. But what exactly are these views? What reasons do we have to think they're true? And what happens when we read comics from these perspectives?

Just the Facts

Answering such questions places us squarely within the area of meta-ethics, the branch of philosophy that takes a step back from our ordinary moral deliberations about what's right and wrong and asks challenging questions about what these very deliberations amount to. What are values in the first place? What, if anything, makes value judgments correct or incorrect?

Here's a way to think about it. In *Superman Returns*, Lex Luthor initiates a plan to "grow" a Kryptonite-laced continent. There's only a slight problem. Doing so is going to wipe out the entire eastern seaboard, killing millions of people. No doubt Superman, Lois Lane, Jimmy Olsen, Perry White, and just about everyone else living in Metropolis would share the following judgments about Lex's action: it's *wrong*; he *oughtn't* have done it; it's *bad*. These judgments are moral judgments. What meta-ethics asks is this: what, if anything, makes these judgments true or false? How this question is answered—and how that answer is defended—will help us see the differences between three competing views about the nature of morality: moral objectivism, moral nihilism, and moral relativism.

In order to understand what these ideas amount to, let's first consider an ordinary, non-moral judgment. Suppose I come to believe that the earth revolves around the sun. And now I wonder what, if anything, makes my judgment true or false. Well, that's easy enough. There are facts that are in some sense independent of us that make my judgment true or false. These are facts involving the way the universe actually is, regardless of what we believe it to be like, or regardless of what standards we've adopted in figuring out what it's like. In this case, the facts are such that my belief is true. If I had believed that the sun revolved around the earth, then my belief would have been false because that's not the way the universe is.

Keeping this in mind, let's understand moral objectivism to be the view that moral facts are a part of the universe, and that these facts make moral judgments true or false in much the same way as facts about celestial bodies make true or false judgments about whether the earth revolves around the sun. Moral objectivists takes these moral facts to be independent of us, just like celestial facts are independent of us; that is, neither kind of facts depend on us for their existence. Simply put, our belief that the earth revolves around the sun doesn't make it so. It's a fact whether we believe it or not. Similarly, moral objectivists think that slavery's being wrong is a fact that doesn't depend on us making it so. It's a fact regardless of what we believe.

Moral nihilism and moral relativism can then be understood in contrast to moral objectivism. Moral nihilism is the view that there aren't any moral facts whatsoever. Nihilists think that moral facts are like facts about unicorns—there aren't any. For the nihilist, it's not a fact that slavery is wrong, nor is it a fact that slavery is right. In contrast, moral relativism is the view that there are moral facts, but they in some way or other depend on us for their existence. Moral relativists don't think that there's a simple fact of the matter that slavery is wrong. Instead, their view is that there are a battery of facts about the moral standing of slavery that depend on the standards of our culture or community. So for relativists, there's the fact that slavery is wrong relative the our culture's current standards, and the fact that slavery isn't wrong relative to our culture's past standards, but there's no absolute fact of the matter about the moral standing of slavery independent of any culture's standards.

Returning to the example we began with, here's how these different views about morality would evaluate Superman's judgment that Lex Luthor's plan to grow a kryptonite-laced continent was wrong. According to moral objectivists, Superman is either correct or incorrect, and it's a fact independent of him and everyone else on the planet—and elsewhere—that makes it so. Moral nihilists would conclude that Superman's judgment is incorrect. What Lex did wasn't wrong—nor was it right—because nothing actually *is* right or wrong. Relativists, for their part, would conclude that Superman's judgment is correct, at least according to the standards he's using. In other words, it's a fact that according to the standards of our culture, what Lex did was wrong. However, Superman's actions could also be wrong relative to the standards of a different culture than our own, real or merely possible, that evaluates an alien incursion of any kind as a greater evil than the massive human casualties it would take to repel that incursion.

We now have before us three competing views about the nature of morality. But which is the right one? Let's turn now to a consideration of some arguments for each of these positions. We'll begin with the most radical of the three, moral nihilism.

Moral Facts Going, Going, Gone

Obviously, moral nihilism runs contrary to our ordinary beliefs. Most of us think that at least some actions are right or wrong. Nihilists, as we've seen, do not. To appreciate just how radical a view this is, consider how a nihilist reads today's comics. For her, the problem isn't that it's difficult to figure out whether Lex Luthor is really a villain, or whether Captain America's actions are morally justified. She takes it that there's *nothing* to figure out here at all! There aren't any moral facts, plain and simple. So for her, Superman isn't a hero, because there aren't any heroes or villains. The Red Skull's pursuit of genocide isn't wrong, because nothing's right or wrong. This is an extreme view. So why should anyone nevertheless think it's correct? Let's look at one of the more famous arguments for moral nihilism, put forward by J.L. Mackie in his book, *Ethics: Inventing Right and Wrong* (Penguin, 1977), to see why.

Mackie argues that if there were such things as moral facts that are independent of us in the way moral objectivists think they are, these facts would have to be quite peculiar and unlike any other kind of facts independent of us. Recall that according to moral objectivists, moral facts are just like celestial facts. Unlike those facts, Mackie argues, if moral facts existed, they would seem to have a strange psychological connection to us. Specifically, once we came to learn the moral facts about certain actions being right or wrong, we'd be moved either to pursue or avoid these actions, and to morally praise or blame them. This is because when we form beliefs about what the right or wrong thing to do is, we usually feel motivated to do or to avoid doing it. If that were correct, there would be a very strange link between moral facts and our motivations. Facts about rightness would have the power to motivate us simply in virtue of our forming beliefs about them. But other facts independent of us don't behave that way. There's nothing motivational associated with forming a belief about the earth revolving around the sun. So this peculiarity associated with moral facts leads Mackie to conclude that they simply don't exist, at least not as moral objectivists understand them. Since he is also unsympathetic to understanding moral facts in a relative way, Mackie concludes that there simply aren't any moral facts at all.

His argument is problematic, though. A quick but important reply is that in fact there are uncontroversial examples of non-moral facts that do seem to have a psychological link to us, and we don't think this means they aren't facts about the world. Consider facts about live wires. When we form the belief that something is a live wire, we're certainly motivated to avoid it. But that doesn't mean the facts about live wires aren't facts about the world that are independent of us. The wire dancing across the ground is live whether I judge it to be or not.

Proponents of Mackie's reasoning will reply that the real strangeness of moral facts is that it's *necessary* that when we form beliefs about them, motivations come along. However, that's not true with facts about live wires. We can easily imagine a world where, for whatever reason, when we form beliefs about live wires, we're not motivated to avoid them. That possibility makes sense. Mackie doesn't think it makes sense to imagine a world where we form beliefs about what's right and wrong, but aren't thereby motivated to pursue or avoid certain actions. However, to the extent that we disagree with Mackie about the whether such possibilities make sense—and it sure seems possible for motivations to come apart from our moral beliefs—we can disagree with his reasons for being a moral nihilist. For now, we'll turn our attention to one very important deficit of moral nihilism, no matter how it's argued. That's the problem of moral nihilism not having any plausible way of doing justice to our moral language or beliefs.

It's Hard to Talk about Nothing

Suppose, for the sake of illustration, that superheroes and supervillains really do exist. That means we have plenty of opportunities to form moral beliefs about the goings-on with our friendly neighborhood heroes and the nefarious villains they confront. We think that Captain America ought to put an end to the Red Skull's pursuit of genocide and we praise him when he does so. We also say things like, "Superman did the right thing by throwing Lex's Kryptonite-laced continent into space."

However, if the moral nihilist is correct, it remains unclear what's happening with our thoughts and speech. One suggestion—the one that Mackie embraces—is to accept the idea that we're all riddled in error. Our moral beliefs are false, and when we make moral claims, we communicate mistakenly. That's because our thoughts and utterances make a claim about the way the world is, but the world isn't that way; they say the world has moral facts, and it doesn't. So when we exclaim, "Lex Luthor is an evil genius," we're saying something false, just as surely as when we exclaim, "Superman did the right thing in stopping him." On this view, almost all of our moral language and thoughts involve nothing but error because there aren't any moral facts to make them true. That, to say the very least, is a very unattractive position to adopt!

Other philosophers who are sympathetic with moral nihilism have tried different solutions to this problem. *Prescriptivists* say that when we utter moral sentences, all we're doing is expressing a command, and commands are neither true nor false. For the prescriptivist, saying "The Red Skull must be stopped" is equivalent to saying "Stop the Red Skull!" This new sentence isn't a factual claim about what we ought to do. It is a simple command, and commands can be obeyed or disobeyed, but they can't be true or false. *Expressivists*, on the other hand, say that when we utter moral sentences, we don't give commands. Instead, we are simply expressing feelings or emotions. For them, saying "The Red Skull has done many wrong things" is just saying something like, "Boo to the Red Skull!"

Clever and interesting as these approaches are, they both suffer from the same problem: they don't make sense of moral disagreement. If you say, "Luthor's tactics are wrong," and I say, "They're perfectly justified," it sure looks like we're disagreeing. Even if we have a conversation to justify our positions to each other, it's completely unclear what is really going on if all we're doing is issuing commands or simply emoting. Moral nihilists owe us a plausible account of the very real phenomena of moral disagreement, and they seem unable to provide one.

Relativism to the Rescue?

Since nihilism is burdened with so many problems, let's turn to moral relativism. Unlike moral nihilists, relativists think there *are* moral facts, but they don't believe there are any *objective* moral facts. In other words, they don't believe that moral facts are like celestial facts—determined just by the way of the universe, independently of us. Rather, they think all moral facts are *subjective*— they're determined by the specific standards of a person or a culture. For example, Superman might think that Lex Luthor ought to be put in jail for his crimes, while Batman might think that he ought to be committed to an asylum. On the relativist's view, both Superman and Batman can be right if they have different standards about what warrants incarceration in a prison. Relative to Superman's standards, Lex ought to be put in jail, and relative to Batman's standards, he ought to be committed. The universe, for its part, doesn't take a stand on this, meaning there's no objective fact of the matter about what ought or ought not be done.

A lot of folks find relativism obvious, but it's not. Here's one bad way of arguing for it. Recall the observations we made earlier about the moral ambiguity found in comic books. It's admittedly very difficult at times for our heroes to determine what the right and wrong thing to do is. Bad guys sometimes act more like the good guys, and vice versa. Even Superman isn't morally infallible. Therefore, there aren't any objective moral facts. Everything's relative.

This is bad reasoning because it moves too quickly from an *epistemological* claim—one having to do with what we can or do know—to a claim about what the moral facts themselves are like. Just because it's difficult to figure out who the good guys and bad guys are, or what the right course of action is, it doesn't follow that there's no such thing as *the* right course of action. Captain America may not know whether he ought to follow Iron Man's lead and embrace the government's unmasking program (see Marvel's *Civil War*), but that doesn't mean there isn't a fact of the matter about what he should do. To claim otherwise would be the equivalent of saying, "Since we can't come to know this fact easily, there must not be a fact to be known." That's pretty arrogant! Also, it runs contrary to much fruitful inquiry. I don't know too many scientists who deny that there's an absolute fact of the matter about the things they investigate, even if they happily acknowledge it's quite difficult to figure out just what that is.

There are better reasons to be a relativist. One is an argument *from charity*. The reasoning goes something like this. It's a fact that different cultures adhere to different, conflicting moral norms. If there's an objective fact of the matter about what is right and wrong, good and bad, then it will turn out that most of these cultures are deeply mistaken when it comes to their moral claims. It seems at best uncharitable and at worst implausible that most cultures could be so wrong about moral affairs. So we ought to adopt the stance that all these cultures are correct in their moral judgments because they are making judgments about what's right and wrong relative to their own norms, and there is no universal set of norms by which to evaluate all others.

Another reason to be a relativist is provided by an argument *to the best explanation*. Here the idea is that the best explanation for persistent, pervasive cultural disagreement about moral issues is that there is no absolute set of moral norms, only relative ones. There is no absolute fact of the matter about whether moral claims are right or wrong, and this fact best explains why persistent, pervasive disagreement continues.

Neither of these arguments are very good, though. Consider first the argument from charity. Suppose we look at the scientific beliefs that cultures throughout history have held—beliefs about the workings of natural forces and things like that. It seems indisputable that most of these cultures were dead wrong about a great many things having to do with the natural world. But saying as much isn't being uncharitable to them. It's merely acknowledging how difficult scientific knowledge is to acquire. It's a *huge* enterprise. Why not think that something similar is true of moral truths? They're out there, but it's going to take a lot of effort on our part to figure them out.

The argument to the best explanation doesn't fare much better. Admittedly, *one* explanation of moral disagreement is that there isn't a fact of the matter to be discovered, but why is that explanation *best*? It seems an *equally good* explanation is that we're just not very skilled at learning about moral facts. Both explanations produce the same outcome, so it's hard to see what makes relativism better as an explanation unless we have already presupposed its correctness. That would certainly be a bad way to argue!

Even if these worries can be addressed, another problem with moral relativism, one we've seen before in a different guise, is that it allows for two persons to appear to be disagreeing without actually disagreeing. Recall Superman's and Batman's views about

Luthor's incarceration. Certainly they seem to be disagreeing, but the relativist claims they aren't. Instead, they're just employing different standards of moral assessment, and relative to those separate standards, each is right. Once more this seems to run contrary to our ordinary belief that people engage in substantive moral disagreement all the time. In this case, it seems like Superman and Batman are disagreeing about what the morally appropriate treatment of Luthor is, plain and simple, not just holding distinct and compatible views about what ought to be done with him given certain standards. Even if we hesitate at this because we're not completely convinced Superman and Batman are having a real disagreement, the worry is that relativism doesn't allow for *any* substantive disagreement, ever, between persons or cultures with different standards. That seems wrong.

A Dose of Moral Objectivity

All of this suggests that moral objectivism is the best option left for us of the ones we've considered. Unlike nihilism and relativism, it makes sense of moral disagreement, and does justice to our moral beliefs and language. It's compatible with many different specific moralities. We might be utilitarians who think that the right actions are the ones that maximize the pleasures and minimize the pains in all creatures capable of experiencing pleasures and pains. Facts about the amount of pleasure and pain a certain action produces in all sentient beings are objective—the universe decides them. Or we might follow Immanuel Kant in believing that we're morally permitted to do those actions that treat people as ends in themselves and not merely as means. Facts about whether people are treated as ends rather than merely as means are objective, too. Moral objectivists aren't committed to claiming that both utilitarians and Kantians are right; these moral views are incompatible, for one thing, and objectivists needn't take a stand on either of them. Rather, the idea is simply that both of these popular moralities, and others as well, assume that there are objective moral facts.

Nonetheless, are there reasons to resist being moral objectivists?

Perhaps the biggest problem that's usually offered is one that has little to do with the merits of the view itself and more to do with the demerits associated with persons holding it. Take Superman. Perhaps surprisingly, many comic book fans loathe Superman precisely because he's a "boy scout," a goody-goody who always fights unquestioningly for truth, justice, and the American way. Superman is someone who thinks there *are* objective moral facts, and he enforces them without wavering. So the worry is that a commitment to moral objectivity leads to arrogance and intolerance.

Now it's certainly true that some people, and perhaps some comic book characters, are moral objectivists who succumb to these vices. But that's a problem with these persons, not the view. Endorsing the idea that there are objective moral facts simply does not warrant attitudes of arrogance and intolerance. Superman can be entirely convinced that there is a right course of action to pursue in his fight against Lex Luthor, and nevertheless remain humble in his assessment of his abilities to correctly arrive at that course of action. He might be a utilitarian, for instance, who despite his mental powers simply can't accurately assess *all* the pleasures and pains that will result from a particular action. Captain America can tirelessly fight to topple the Red Skull's Aryan ambitions—convinced that it's an objective fact that genocide is wrong—without slinging his shield at non-violent white supremacists, despite his understandable distaste of their views. Intolerance is not forced upon Superman or Captain America by moral objectivism. If they choose intolerance, that's a choice they make all on their own.

So although the world of comic books is painted these days in many shades of gray, we needn't view this moral complexity as pointing to relativism or nihilism. These narratives don't force us to embrace the idea that there really aren't heroes and villains at each end of the moral spectrum, or that what they do isn't objectively right or wrong. Instead, we can read the Modern Age of Comics as inviting us to acknowledge that objective moral truths are an extremely challenging thing to arrive at. If it's tough even for super-heroes and supervillains to get straight, how much more difficult must it be for us? We should therefore look to the likes of Superman and Captain American as moral exemplars because their struggles to wrest moral knowledge from the world prove no less heroic and difficult than their physical struggles in battling the bad guys.

8
Mojo's Tribe Has Spoken

J.J. SYLVIA IV and SEAN WALTERS

Mojo first appeared in 1985 in the pages of the *Longshot* limited series as the leader of a parallel universe, ever so humbly named the Mojoverse, whose entire culture is based on the television studio system. In Mojoworld, whoever gets the highest ratings is the undisputed ruler, and Mojo is the best at what he does. He produces violent shows that are eagerly consumed by Mojoworld's obese, television-addicted citizens, the Spineless Ones. Once Mojo realized that the X-Men could be an unlimited resource for his televised battles, he began kidnapping them and coercing them to compete for his audience's amusement. It's not hard to see why Mojo has become a popular recurring X-villain—he's relentless, heartless, and endlessly entertaining. For our purposes, however, he's more than that because he allows us to investigate an influential industry in our own society.

Mojoworld can be understood as a metaphor for the very real television culture of the past two or three decades. Mojo's tireless efforts to keep his society from boredom mirror the television industry's push for fresh and exciting programming each new season. These fresh and exciting ideas have increasingly become reality shows, many of which are quite similar to Mojo's gladiator-style contests. Sure, the comparison between Mojo and our own television producers is not a perfect metaphor, but the similarities are interesting.

It's very easy to dismiss Mojo as a villain confined to the pages of a comic book because in the real world, things are always a bit more complex and a bit less certain. Television stations are rarely vilified for seeking to increase their ratings as Mojo is, but like any

other television producer, Mojo produces entertainment that people want. In the *X-Men* animated series episode "Mojovision," Mojo
makes it clear that the audience doesn't want to see things like
peace, or freedom, or good government. They want blood and guts
and love and hate. In the Mojoverse, good ratings are generated by
showing the audience what *they want to see*. Mojo simply produces
whatever will satisfy that desire, and his ratings and power increase
the more he does so.

If the audience didn't want to see blood and guts and love and
hate, then they probably wouldn't watch those programs, and
Mojo's ratings would decrease. In other words, Mojo would have
absolutely no incentive to produce those shows. Yet both in Mojo's
universe and in our own, people continue to watch these types of
shows, so studios continue to produce them. Mojo's defense of
himself is that he, the same as our own television studios, is just
innocently serving a public which is already immoral.

An Insidious Fix

Surely such a defense only acknowledges part of the story. Part of
Mojo's villainy is that he takes people against their will and forces
them to compete in dangerous and life-threatening situations.
People are actually being physically or psychologically harmed by
the production of his entertainment. So we can also object to
Mojo's methods as distinctly villainous. Although there can be dangerous situations on some of our own reality programs, they are
rarely ever life-threatening. Furthermore, all of the participants
agree to participate, so our own situation in those respects is distinctly different.

Mojo might still claim that the differences between his methods
and those of our own reality television programs are not as great
as we imagine. In their book *Shooting People: Adventures in Reality
TV* (Verso, 2003), Sam Brenton and Reuben Cohen identify problematic areas of reality television. The book begins with Sinisa
Savija, a participant on the reality show *Expedition Robinson* filmed
in 1997. His wife claims that he was a happy and stable person
before filming, but shortly after he was the first person voted off of
the island, he threw himself under a train because he feared the
show would make him look like a fool. *Expedition Robinson* was
certainly not as directly responsible for the death of its participant
as a show aired by Mojo might be, but the authors and Sinisa's

widow believe that it was Sinisa's participation in the show that led to his death.

Sinisa's case is obviously extreme. Since 1997 there have been many reality television shows with many participants who felt just fine after the whole experience. However, the entire point of much reality television is to put people in situations that inflict some type of physical or emotional duress, and then broadcast how well or, hopefully for the ratings, how poorly people deal with it. Whether it's as simple as living with strangers or trying to survive on a remote island, the point is surely not to make life *better* for the participants, even if one (and only one) of them will win a valuable prize. If the rule is that we instigate intense conflict for entertaining television, that might as well be Mojo's motto as well.

That Ethical Mojo

What about Mojo's use of unwilling participants? If we say that Mojo *shouldn't* use unwilling participants, we could mean at least two things. First, we could mean that it is unwise and counter to his goals to do that. Mojo's goal is to increase his viewership and his power, but if the Spineless Ones refused to watch any show that forces competition among unwilling prisoners, we could say Mojo *shouldn't* capture people and force them to compete since it would cause his viewership to decrease. However, this is only a practical reason with no ethical concerns.

There is a second use of the word *should*, a moral use. If we say that a serial killer *shouldn't* kill people, we don't mean that he shouldn't do this because it interferes with some goal of his. We mean that morality requires that he shouldn't kill other people. It's in this sense that we say Mojo *shouldn't* capture people and force them to compete in his shows. X-Man Jean Grey expresses a similar sentiment: "Scott and Storm are human beings. You can't destroy them just to keep people amused" ("Mojovision," *X-Men* episode written by Brooks Wachtel).

Jean's claim is not that the Spineless Ones won't be amused or entertained by destroying Scott and Storm. Instead, she is claiming that Mojo *shouldn't* destroy them as an ethical matter.

Is Jean right? Methods of ethical analysis vary, but Mojo's arguments tend toward a kind of simple utilitarianism. The British philosopher generally considered the father of utilitarianism is Jeremy Bentham (1748–1832). Bentham believed it was possible to calculate the amount of overall pleasure or pain that would come from each possible action. In its most basic form, utilitarianism says that the ethical or correct action is the one that generates the greatest good, understood as pleasure or the avoidance of pain, for the greatest number of people. Given the choice between two actions, you weigh the net benefit each action would cause for the people affected, and then choose whichever brings the most pleasure or the least pain.

Mojo appeals to the aggregated pleasure of millions in his viewing audience to justify his capturing a few X-Men and forcing them to participate in his show. If he doesn't capture them, the X-Men will surely avoid a painful experience and Mojo's viewers will not have the pleasure their entertainment provides. On the other hand, if Mojo does capture the X-Men, they will experience some pain, but Mojo and millions of his viewers will experience pleasure from the entertainment their combat provides.

What gives Mojo's analysis traction is the basic premise of value as desire-satisfaction. In other words, we all work to satisfy basic desires such as food, shelter, and clothing. After that, we work to satisfy other desires, entertainment being one of them. For utilitarians and others who see value as desire-satisfaction, this is the source of meaning and value in life. So if this is so, why can't Mojo claim he's just helping people fulfill their desires in the most efficient way possible? We certainly want that kind of efficiency in military decisions and public health matters because it will minimize pain and mortality (negative value or disvalue), so perhaps we should endorse Mojo's actions after all!

Better a Man Dissatisfied than a Spineless One Satisfied

John Stuart Mill (1806–1873) was another early defender of utilitarian ethics, but he most likely wouldn't agree with the ethical analysis we've laid out so far. Mill famously distinguished between what he called higher and lower pleasures by saying that it is better to be a man dissatisfied than a pig satisfied, and better to be Socrates dissatisfied than a man satisfied. Mill's distinction reminds us that humans can enjoy intellectual pleasures in a way that pigs cannot. We can appreciate a painting or a song in a way pigs never could. Moreover, even among people there are differences. Socrates's pursuit of wisdom allows him to enjoy intellectual pleasures more deeply than many of his countrymen, and so he too will live a better life on utilitarian grounds. Mill argues in each case that higher pleasures are better than lower pleasures, and thus makes the crucial point that utilitarian reasoning should be mindful of quality over quantity.

If what separates higher and lower pleasures is a qualitative distinction, then Mill's contribution to utilitarianism might seem vulnerable. Think about how many more are the number of people enjoying Heath Ledger's portrayal of the Joker in *The Dark Knight* than those who are struggling to understand Plato's allegory of the cave. In Mill's view, those who read Plato will be better off, but how can he support the argument that reading Plato is the higher pleasure? The Spineless Ones would tell us that they much prefer Mojo's death sports to whatever pleasures might be had by reading Plato. So why do we think that the pleasure they get from Mojo's programs is actually a lower pleasure?

Mill responds by introducing a certain kind of person known as the "competent judge." For Mill, only those people capable of experiencing both higher and lower pleasures are qualified to make judgments about which pleasures are higher than others. Seeking higher pleasures cultivates the senses with which one experiences them, and therefore allows one to make the necessary fine distinctions. In that way, cultivating the ability to distinguish higher pleasures is like cultivating a plant which must be nurtured in order to survive. Thus, to know what pleasures are higher pleasures we must look to the individual who can get pleasure both from watching the latest action movie *and* from reading Plato, and that person can tell us which pleasure is of a higher quality. Mill believes that on the whole the competent judges will answer that activities like philosophical discussion always produce a higher quality of pleasure than just watching television, and that even watching television is better than just having one's basic physical needs satisfied.

Remember Mojo's claim that many Spineless Ones enjoy his programs at the cost of only a few X-Men's pain? When we consider that simple utilitarian defense in light of Mill's distinction between higher and lower pleasures, things begin to look a little different. Because the Spineless Ones refuse to seek higher pleasures, they will have lost their ability to enjoy them and (more importantly) to distinguish them as well. The pleasure they take in watching Mojo's blood-and-guts programming is a lower pleasure, and although utilitarianism requires a person to act in ways that create the greatest *overall* happiness, Mojo's utilitarian defense rings hollow.

Without these television shows, the Spineless Ones might go on to pursue better or higher quality activities that bring with them higher pleasures. Imagine that without the television show, each Spineless One reads a book and begins to discover the higher intellectual pleasures of reading. This would be a higher pleasure than they get from watching the X-Men do battle on Mojo's programs. No matter how many Spineless Ones enjoy the lower pleasures of Mojo's programming, the utilitarian value of those pleasures is still inferior to the value of the higher pleasures Mojo's captivity denies the X-Men, and certainly inferior to the higher pleasures the Spineless Ones could seek as an alternative to watching blood-sports. Seen in this light, a more thorough reading of utilitarian principles suggests that the best action for everyone is not to capture the X-Men after all.

Discussions about utilitarianism can easily become more complex than the explanations we've outlined here. Some people argue there are problems with Mill's distinction between higher and lower pleasures. Others believe that utilitarianism is much too demanding. For example, if we must always increase the overall happiness, we must constantly be working to improve the situation of those who are worse off than we are, as long as we have the means. So while there are certainly other issues that could be raised, the main point is that utilitarianism is a very useful way of explaining why and how Mojo's actions are unethical. Can we say the same about our own universe's reality television producers?

It might seem strange or even counterproductive to discuss desires and satisfaction as a part of ethics. Even Mill's attempt at an objective argument becomes subjective and almost circular with his inclusion of the competent judges: competent judges are defined by their ability to appreciate higher and lower pleasures, but higher pleasures are defined by competent judges. Without an objective account of qualitative differences in satisfaction and desire, we are no closer to proof of Mojo's villainy. Because of the subjectivity of these desire satisfaction models, many consider them to be relativistic, meaning the correct moral action for any situation could vary from person to person. However, this is not necessarily the case. In the next section we will see how a system of desire satisfaction might be understood objectively.

Moral Realism

Philosophers like Peter Railton defend a way that desires can factor into a form of moral realism. Let's consider a non-moral example first. We said in our exploration of "should" earlier that a decision is good for a person if it would satisfy an objective interest of theirs. For example, if it's in your interest not to have the flu this year, and getting a flu shot can prevent that, then it's good for you to get a flu shot.

But we don't know everything. You might not know that flu shots are available, or you might believe they'll make you sick. Either way, you don't desire a flu shot. To get an objective account of the situation, Railton appeals to an ideal advisor, You+. You+ has complete knowledge about you and your environment and is fully rational. We could then ask You+ what he wants normal you to want. Does You+ want you to want a flu shot? His answer is the objective good for you.

Railton suggests that what differentiates moral behavior from non-moral behavior is that moral behavior concerns the interests of more than one person. To get an objective account, You+ must equally consider the desires of the other ideal advisors. The morally correct action is the action your ideal advisor would approve after taking into account the desires of all other ideal agents.

How would this work in the Mojoverse? We'd need to see what action fully rational and aware agents would approve for all of society. If this were a non-moral situation, Mojo+ might advise that Mojo's actions are good. Because this is a moral situation (that is, because the X-Men's interests are affected by Mojo's decision), Mojo+ must advocate an action that takes into account the desires of the X-Men+. Whatever the outcome, we can at least be fairly sure that the X-Men+ (and so Mojo+) would have the desire to keep the X-Men out of deadly combat, which would make Mojo's forcing the X-Men into combat an immoral act.

Railton's system is attractive in that while it doesn't mandate a one-size-fits-all morality, it also doesn't support a completely relative morality. That is, the moral choice doesn't rely solely on the desires of the person making the decision; it takes account of the informed desires of others. So unlike many relativist moralities, Railton's doesn't let a person's personal desires exempt them from moral obligation. Therefore, one could objectively claim that Mojo should not capture the X-Men or inflict such television upon the

Spineless Ones. Obviously many philosophical issues can be discussed regarding Mojo, but we should step back for a moment and ask if any of the questions we've discussed have a bearing on our own lives.

Business as Usual

Comics have frequently prompted us to reflect on ourselves and our culture. They often touch on our concerns, fears, and hopes, and we therefore might see Mojo as a metaphor for the extremes to which reality television might one day resort. Obviously television is not bad in and of itself—because television shows can (and frequently do) help us experience higher pleasures. Like literature, television is a medium capable of generating both high and low art, and it is our task to seek its best material before we, like the Spineless Ones, lose the ability to distinguish it from the worst.

Should recent trends in recent reality television give us reason for concern? MTV's *Real World* has gone from a simple social experiment to a casting process that purposefully picks personalities who will clash over petty and trivial matters. Fox's *Temptation Island* forced participants to watch videos that had been intentionally edited to imply that their partners had cheated on them in cases when they hadn't. All of this programming aims to generate ratings by showcasing others' psychological duress for our viewing pleasure. If what makes Mojo a supervillain is the programming he creates in service of the Spineless Ones' low pleasures, then our own reality television programming should suggest that villains of that kind might not be so fantastic after all.

Phase Three

Taking Over the World

9

Why Doctor Doom Is Better than The Authority

ANDREW TERJESEN

One of the great comic book continuity controversies (akin to whether Batman ever caught his parents' killer or whether Superman's parents should have died before he became Superman) is the dispute over what Doctor Doom looks like under that mask.

Jack Kirby is reported to have said that under Doom's mask there is only "a tiny scar on his cheek."[1] John Byrne showed Doom's face as ravaged in *Fantastic Four 258*. In the *Books of Doom* mini-series, Ed Brubaker followed Kirby's lead and left Doom's face to our imagination. Given Doom's penchant for robot doubles, it's entirely possible for both Kirby and Byrne's Doom to be a part of the Marvel Universe.

A tougher question is whether Doom is evil all the way through or whether he possesses a higher, nobler aspect. In his first appearance in *Fantastic Four #5* (and for several years after that) Doctor Doom was portrayed as a stereotypical megalomaniac who wanted to conquer the world. His reasons for fighting the Fantastic Four are relics of the Silver Age: he saw the Four as an obstacle to his world conquest and he blamed Reed Richards for his disfigurement.

In *Fantastic Four Annual #2*, Victor von Doom's story was fleshed out and we learned of the harsh upbringing he had—growing up a gypsy, having lost his mother (later revealed to have been trapped in the afterlife after she made a deal with Mephisto), his father killed by the tyrannical ruler of Latveria and struggling with the oppressive Latverian regime. It's revealed even later that Doom

---

[1] Arlen Schumer, *The Silver Age of Comic Book Art,* Collector's Press, 2003, p. 77.

is concerned for his subjects' welfare (for example in *Supervillain Team-Up* #11). The transformation of Doom into a complex mega-lomaniac with noble qualities was completed during John Byrne's run on the *Fantastic Four*.

As Doom tells the Fantastic Four (in front of a completely dev-astated Latveria): "When Victor von Doom ruled here, Latveria was the richest, most prosperous nation in all Europe. No man or woman was without employment. No child went to bed hungry. Until Zorba's followers stirred up discontent in factions of the pop-ulace. There was no crime, no civil strife" (*Fantastic Four #246*). In fact Doom lays the blame for the devastation at the feet of the Fantastic Four because they sided with those rebels. Maybe it would be too much to think of Dr. Doom as a superhero, but it does suggest that he is not devoid of good qualities.

Doom's behavior seems to embody what the French call *"noblesse oblige"* which translates as "nobility obligates," but which the Oxford English Dictionary defines as "privilege entails to respon-sibility." Really it's a fancy word that embodies Spider-Man's motto "with great power, comes great responsibility," but the French ver-sion retains a delectable snobbery we academics cannot resist. Doom also seems to display a kind of magnanimity, which is very similar to *noblesse oblige*. Literally "magnanimity" means "greatsouled."

The Greek philosopher Aristotle (384–322 B.C.E.) listed magna-nimity as one of the main virtues. He describes it as follows, "a per-son is thought to be great-souled if he claims much and deserves much; he who claims much without deserving it is foolish" (*Nicomachean Ethics*, line 1123a1). *Noblesse oblige* refers to one's obligations because of one's station in life, but it does not demand the superior qualities of magnanimity. However, *noblesse oblige* comes from the assumption that those in positions of power are morally and intellectually superior beings. Certainly Doom sees himself that way.

The Virtues of Doom

For some people, the idea that a supervillain bent on world con-quest would allow themselves to be constrained by a code of honor (or possess a virtue, even if it's just magnanimity) seems ridiculous. In the "Unthinkable" story arc, Mark Waid portrayed Doom as anything but a noble villain. In his proposal for the series, Waid argued that the truism that Victor von Doom is, despite his villainy, a noble man is absolute crap. A man whose entire motivating force is jealousy is ridiculously petty, not grandly noble. Yes, Doom is *regal*, and yes, whenever possible, Doom likes to *act* as if he possesses great moral character, because to him that's what great men *have* . . . [Doom] *would tear the head off a newborn baby and eat it like an apple while his mother watched if it would somehow prove he were smarter than Reed.* (From Waid's "The Fantastic Four Manifesto," found in *Fantastic Four Volume 1: Imaginauts*)

Waid's take on Doom is rooted in his interpretation of Doom as being motivated primarily by jealousy and that this jealousy is not limited by honor. But it's not always clear that this is Doom's main reason for doing things. It's just as likely that he is moved by a desire for control or order (which requires rules), a belief that he is the only person smart enough to have power, or a real concern for those who have shown him loyalty in his very tumultuous life. Admittedly, Doom's concern for those who are loyal to him is probably equivalent to the regard many of us give our pets. Doom does not view their needs as equivalent to his. If he had to choose between saving them and furthering a master plan, they would probably lose out every time. As long as nothing else demands his attention, Doom will act on their behalf. It's not the same as Spider-man's penchant for self-sacrifice, but it seems praiseworthy nonetheless.

Waid's take on Doom reflects a commonly-held belief that it is not possible for someone to ever really be good if they are generally a bad person. It's hard to believe that a villain like Doom, who's willing to kill people to achieve his aims, is capable of abiding by a set of rules that limits what he can achieve. Plus, it seems strange that someone like Doom could understand the importance of honor in a duel when he sees no intrinsic value in life. Moral philosophers refer to this idea as the "Unity of the Virtues." Thomas Aquinas (1224–1274 C.E.) was a medieval philosopher who thought that Aristotle had gotten it mostly right. As Aquinas explains,

> discretion belongs to prudence, rectitude to justice, moderation to temperance, and strength of mind to fortitude. . . . strength of mind is not commended as virtuous, if it be without moderation or rectitude or discretion. (*Summa Theologica*, I–II, q. 65)

Aquinas's point is that it is impossible to be truly just if you lack the courage to do the just thing when it is dangerous or unpopular. Similarly, if you can't control your desires (for food, sex, or even power) then there will come a time when you will choose what you desire over the right thing to do.

The "Unity of Virtues" thesis is more than just the claim that you can only be truly good if you possess all the virtues. No one really seems to dispute that. Someone who possesses all the virtues would be better than someone with fewer virtues, which means that no matter how you define it, the best person to be is someone with all the virtues. What's really interesting about the "Unity of the Virtues" is the way it challenges the idea that Doom has a praise-worthy characteristic, such as magnanimity. Waid seems to be argu-ing that you can't call Doom honorable or magnanimous because his behavior is not restrained by other virtues, like compassion or justice. Aristotle (who subscribed to the "Unity of Virtues" thesis) seems to be in Waid's corner, because he says that magnanimity is the

> crowning ornament of the virtues: it enhances their greatness, and it cannot exist without them. Hence it is hard to be truly great souled, for greatness of soul is impossible without moral nobility. (*Nicomachean Ethics*, line 1124a1)

But maybe this sets the bar too high. It's one thing to say that we're better people if we have all the virtues, but it's something else to say that there is no such thing as magnanimity if all the rel-evant virtues are not also present. If we follow the "Unity of the Virtues" thesis, we deny that any virtue can be understood apart from all the other virtues. When Doom refuses to kick someone while they are down or delays turning against someone because he has made a promise, it seems clear that this is a magnanimous action on his part. We don't need to see that he has all the other virtues in order to recognize that he has that quality. Someone might object that Doom acts *like* a magnanimous person, but is not *actually* magnanimous because he lacks all the virtues. But if we push that too far, then no one is ever magnanimous, and that just seems contrary to common sense. And, as the philosopher Philippa Foot has pointed out, the "Unity of the Virtues" thesis depends on the assumption that having a virtue means you *always* act accord-ing to that virtue. But that's like saying Doom is only a genius if he never makes a mistake.

A Finer World . . . at Any Cost?

The state of Latveria is a small example of what the world would be like if Doom succeeded in conquering it. It is a world in which the ills of human existence have all been eradicated and the price of this achievement is that one must regard Doom as one's master. This is a pretty hefty price because it means to deferring to Doom's judgment in all things and (as we'll discuss later) surrendering most of the basic freedoms people cherish. In *Emperor Doom*, Dr. Doom uses the Purple Man to enslave the will of the world and then goes about setting his policies in place. He ends global conflicts and street crime, boosts world food production, brings an end to Apartheid, and enacts policies that cause an investment boom worldwide. Although his means might be deplorable, Doom's overall political goals might seem pretty desirable.

In an alternate universe visited by the Exiles, Victor von Doom is a hero who has created a utopian society by once again interfering with people's free will. As the Reed Richards of that parallel world notes, Victor von Doom will act "believing with all his heart and soul that everything he does is for the best" (*Exiles #96*). *What If . . . Secret Wars* (2008) presents yet another alternate universe where Doom uses cosmic power to force people into a better world.

Other magnanimous supervillains also seem to be acting with the best of intentions. Lex Luthor has recently been portrayed as someone who opposes Superman because he views him as a great threat to humanity. In *Lex Luthor: Man of Steel,* he engages in an imaginary conversation with Superman, saying:

> Truth? That's in the teller. Just calmly massaged words that very well may be nothing but carefully finessed lies. Justice? Justice belongs to the judge, who sits above those who put him there because they can't trust themselves. And the American Way? It constantly evolves out of something that proves to be true and a lie, just and more—all men are created equal. . . . You are not a man. . . . I see something no man can ever be. I see the end. The end of our potential. The end of our achievements. The end of our dreams. You are my nightmare.

And he could have added, the end of magnanimity. No human being could think of themselves as great-souled when compared to Superman. Coming from Lex Luthor, it sounds like the words of a wounded ego, but that concern about the danger of superhumans to human existence is echoed by Superman himself in *Kingdom Come*.

That said, magnanimous supervillains are still unmistakably villainous because without other virtues to restrain them, they look for ways to bend the rules so that their admirable qualities don't interfere with their nefarious goals. One example frequent almost to the point of cliché is the promise not to harm the heroes while they have a common enemy, but as soon as the threat is ended, the "magnanimous" supervillain shoots his "allies" from behind.

On this issue it seems that the "Unity of Virtues" thesis has a point. Superheroes in the Silver Age recognized that there were rules they could not bend, but the idea that some rules can't be bent or broken by "real" superheroes seems to be disappearing along with the bright line between hero and villain. In *Identity Crisis*, it was revealed that the Justice League was altering the memories and behaviors of criminals (and even Batman). However, the first superheroes to *really* push the old rules aside were The Authority.

The Authority embrace the idea that the great responsibility of bearing superpowers requires a more proactive than reactive posture. Accordingly, The Authority didn't spend time waiting for crimes or disasters to occur when they could be changing the world for the better instead. With their extraordinary power, they could achieve extraordinary good, and relative to that good, how could they be fettered by old-fashioned prohibitions against killing people or violating political sovereignty?

At the end of their first mission, Jack Hawksmoor comments: "How many people would've died if we hadn't been here? It's not a great answer, I know; but it's the best there is. We saved more people than we killed" (*Authority* #4). In successive adventures, the Authority kept pushing the boundaries of what they would do to change the world. They overthrow (and execute) an oppressive dictator (*Authority* #13). The Engineer defends their actions by appeal to the rhetorical question, "How can you expect us to save people from extraterrestial threats, but turn a blind eye when genocide is being perpetrated by Earth-bound dictators?" Midnighter more succinctly puts it this way: "The twenty-first century is a bad time to be a bastard, children."

One might still try and argue that there is an important difference between world-conquering supervillains like Doom and proactive heroes like The Authority. Maybe the difference is that Doom is trying to conquer the world in order to do what he thinks is best, while the Authority is merely trying to punish those who have been abusing the world. However, the Authority themselves (in the *Coup d'État* miniseries) take over the United States after the US government completely obliterates Florida while experimenting with inter-dimensional travel.

What seems clear in both cases then is that the Authority *and* Doctor Doom have set themselves up as the ones who know what is best for the world, and we'd better listen to them because they have the power to make us do what they want. They are willing to weigh the good and bad consequences of their actions and do what produces the most good, no matter how abhorrent the bad consequences might seem. Both seem to operate on the assumption that positive change in the world will come at a price, and this is in stark contrast to the "old-fashioned" Silver Age superheroes who refused to accept that they should do anything less than make everything work out for the best. The Silver Age hero wanted to embody all the virtues in each action, but the Authority seems quite content to realize one virtue at the expense of others.

The Burdens of Genius

Doom would have us believe that the price of peace and prosperity is cheaper than that. As Doom spins it: "All I took from the people was a single freedom . . . the freedom to commit evil" (*Fantastic Four #247*). In Doom's mind this makes sense, he knows best and so acts that contradict his judgment are evil. If one chooses to disobey Doom, the punishment is harsh, and that can be quite a deterrent in Latveria.

Doom is being a bit simplistic here. The freedom to commit evil can only be removed if we carefully observe everyone's actions and enforce an unquestioned standard of behavior. This means sacrificing a number of freedoms, including privacy and the ability to disagree with Doom.

Both Doom's actions and those of The Authority remove humanity's ability to choose its own destiny. This was Lex's fear about Superman. With so much more power than all of us put together, Superman, Doom, and The Authority could actually exercise significant control over everyone on the planet, almost as though we were children being directed by the paternal will of a superhuman parent. Presumably we think we're entitled to treat children this way because they are not ready for adult responsibility, but Doom and the Authority are only more powerful, they are not *morally* superior to everyone else (except in their own minds).

What makes us equal to these superhumans is that we all possess a capacity for free choice. The idea that freedom is an essential part of who we are as moral beings was the backbone of Jack Kirby's *Fourth World Saga* (and its spiritual descendant in Grant Morrison's *Final Crisis*). Darkseid seeks the Anti-Life Equation because it would give him the power to control everyone's minds. Kirby's New Gods oppose Darkseid, and they put it nicely in *The Forever People* Vol 1, #5: "Without independent will—you might just as well be a robot!" Our ability to make choices separates us from everything else in the universe, and Doom and the Authority have no more right to choose for us than we have to choose for them.

But our would-be Super-Overlords can rightly ask, What's so special about freedom? Freedom may be nice, but people can freely hurt others, steal from them, and even kill them. As Hawkeye says to Captain America at the end of *Emperor* Doom: "We've done humankind the greatest favor in history—or we've done it the greatest damage." Do the mixed benefits of freedom *really* outweigh the social goods their coercion would secure? After all, very few people support the idea that we should be *completely* free to do whatever we want, and our laws accordingly limit the exercise of unconditional or unlimited freedom. Most philosophers agree with John Stuart Mill (1806–1873) who argued that "The liberty of the individual must be thus far limited; he must not make himself a nuisance to other people" (*On Liberty*, 1859, Chapter 3).

However some philosophers argue that the law should be paternalistic forcing us to do (or not do) things for our own good even if no one else is affected by our actions. The philosopher Gerald Dworkin justifies paternalism in cases where the amount of harm one might do to oneself is great and the chances of reversing the damage are small ("Paternalism," *The Monist* 56, 1972, pp. 64–84). For example, if you don't wear your seatbelt you could become permanently paralyzed if you got into an accident. For this reason, most states have laws that require you to "Click it or ticket." On the other hand, many household appliances are capable of inflicting minor injuries, but because these will usually heal in a few days, the law requires only a manufacturer's warning for consumer safety.

Most of the time the world is not poised on such a danger-ous precipice that the kind of paternalism Doom and The Authority practice would be necessary. In the graphic novel *Watchmen*, the hero turned "supervillain" Ozymandias deter-mines that humanity is heading towards extinction in nuclear conflict, and so he orchestrates a massive conspiracy, that kills millions of people, to avert global disaster. He doesn't conquer the world, but he does engage in paternalistic coercion to force the world to co-operate.

Most social ills could probably be fixed if we really paid atten-tion to them. Doom, Luthor, and even The Authority may think of themselves as those who know best, but until they've convinced the six billion fellow human beings with whom they share the world that their vision is right, it's more likely that the most they can hope for is compliance rather than principled agreement, and the least they should expect is that they'll raise whole generations of anarchists in Guy Fawkes masks as well.

You might point out that there's a big difference between fight-ing people who you think are dangerous (as The Authority did) and using the Purple Man to enslave the Earth. This is true, but The Authority's power makes it more likely that people would choose whatever the Authority wants for fear of getting beaten up. This might not be as big a deal if we could be sure that no one would ever use the power of the Authority to further their own agenda, but we have no guarantee that they are correct in their perceptions of what is best for us.

The Noble's Bond

Insofar as they are acting paternalistically, even with the noblest goals, Dr. Doom, the Authority, and even Iron Man (during the Civil War) are taking the role of the villain. Tony Stark's behavior in getting the Registration Act passed and then enforcing it is another example of how Doom can seem like a good guy in com-parison. It is implied in *Civil War: Frontline* that Tony took control of Norman Osborn with nanites in order to provoke sympathy for the Registration Act. And then there are the things he admits to doing: cloning Thor, creating a prison in the Negative Zone in a fla-grant violation of human rights, manipulating Peter Parker, and so forth. What separates Iron Man from Doom and The Authority, and makes him a real superhero, is that after *Secret Invasion* he seems to realize that he crossed a line and takes steps to avoid doing it again in the future.

Doom, The Authority, and Iron Man place their moral judgment above that of their moral peers only because they have the power to do so, but the world is not so endangered or unable to turn things around that such paternalism could be independently justified. However, while they may all be villains, they are not equally villainous. Dr. Doom appears to be less villainous than the Authority because his magnanimity limits how far he will exercise his control. Say what you want about Doom, but it seems unbelievable that Doom would flood all of Italy, destroy a nine-year-old boy's psyche, or kill a sleeping infant in order to achieve his goals. By contrast, The Authority are unwilling to limit themselves by anything more than the expedients of cold utility. If the opportunity presented itself, I doubt they would even wait until they had fulfilled their end of the bargain before shooting their "allies" in the back.

Maybe I'm overestimating Dr. Doom by taking him at his word that he is not petty, but at least he appears to be playing by some rules. Doom's power is so great that he could probably get what he wanted no matter what, but his desire to appear, if not actually be), magnanimous keeps him from exercising it to its fullest extent. By contrast, the members of the Authority do not have the qualities that limit the extent to which they exercise their power over others, and their apparent lack of magnanimity could (under the right circumstances) make them more dangerous to us than any supervillain who was willing to play by at least *some* of the rules.

10
Marvel's Recent Unpleasantness

LIBBY BARRINGER

We aren't generally alarmed when superheroes do big, dangerous, knock-your-socks-off deeds. Part of what makes a superhero, well, super, is that they can do things the average person can't. They are stronger, faster, and—because it's an unfair world—usually better looking than the rest of us, too. What's more, we love them for it! We love it when Batman crashes through a skylight, when Spider-Man swoops off a skyscraper, or when Storm's eyes go white and the sky goes black. We even, despite his protests to the contrary, really love it when Bruce Banner gets angry.

For a moment, however, consider what it would be like to live in a world where an ordinary person on the street could have as much power in her pinkie as a small H-bomb. In comic books, just as in real life, people come in all shapes, sizes, and motivations. More often than not, super-folk are simply ordinary people with extraordinary genetics. Like ordinary people, it's not always easy to peg these characters down as strictly good or bad. They're flawed. They make mistakes. Sometimes, even acting with the best intentions, their dealings have terrible consequences.

In the opening pages of Marvel's *Civil War,* a team of reality-TV superheroes provoke the villain Nitro into detonating the equivalent of a nuclear explosion just outside of an elementary school in Stamford, Connecticut. Hundreds are killed, many of them children. These events lead to the expedited passage of a superhero registration act, and divides the superhero community in two. Tony Stark (Iron Man), Reed Richards (Mister Fantastic of the Fantastic Four), and Hank Pym (Yellowjacket) lead the pro-registration camp, squaring off against Steve Rogers (Captain America) on the other side. Other heroes are torn between these, and by the end of the mini-series the Marvel Universe is transformed. Stark is appointed head of the government security force, S.H.I.E.L.D., Spider-Man leads a radical underground opposition, and Captain America is in chains.

Stamford and the State of Nature

Central to the *Civil War* conflict is one of the oldest questions of political philosophy: is it better to be free, or better to be safe? The way the Marvel community responds to this question is best understood through the eyes of Thomas Hobbes.

Hobbes (1588–1679) is best known for his depiction of the "state of nature," a description of what mankind is like outside of civil society. In this state of nature, all men and women are born equal—but this isn't some rosy vision of equal dignity or worth. The equality Hobbes has in mind is a kind of equal vulnerability. Sure, some people are born stronger than others, some faster or smarter; but everyone is capable of being killed—even the strongest person has to sleep sometime.

If this seems grim, I'm sorry. It gets worse. Just as all people are equally vulnerable, they're also equally free. However freedom here means "unrestrained." Individuals have the right to preserve their lives and welfare through any means possible, including harming, killing, or enslaving others. Nobody is trustworthy in the state of nature because everyone is driven by fear. The state of nature is a state of war, and as Hobbes writes, the life of man is "solitary, poor, nasty, brutish, and short."

This may sound preposterous, but take a moment to consider the context in which it was written. In Hobbes's lifetime alone England went through civil war, the beheading of a king, the implosion of a republic, and numerous religious conflicts. All of these were bloody. The state of nature wasn't simply an imaginary place for Hobbes. It was a condition that mankind might revert to at any time, and in fact already existed. He writes:

> It may seem strange . . . that Nature should thus dissociate, and render men apt to invade and destroy one another. . . . Let him therefore consider with himself—when taking a journey, he arms himself, and seeks to go well accompanied; when going to sleep, he locks his doors; when even in his house he locks his chests; and this when he

knows there be laws and public officers armed to revenge all injuries shall be done him. . . . Does he not there as much accuse mankind by his actions, as I do by my words? (Hobbes, *Leviathan*, Cambridge University Press 1996, p. 89. I've modernized the spelling.)

Hobbes's point here is pretty straightforward: we can't be sure how other people will behave, and we don't trust them to act in our best interests. Even in the actual world, with a government in place, we're plagued by the uncertainty and fear that define the state of nature.

How does this relate to Marvel's *Civil War*? If this is how we act around each other as boring, average, and comparatively lame human beings, consider how it would be if strangers could blow up buildings with a thought.

According to Hobbes, all the members of the Marvel universe are equal to one another, super powers or no (every super has his kryptonite). Yet what guarantee do Marvel denizens have that those with super powers will exercise them judiciously? The short answer is, they don't. Plenty of super villains gleefully reject the mantra that with great power comes great responsibility. Simply by existing as powerful, unrestrained beings with the ability to inflict harm, super villains recreate, even embody, the state of nature. Through their actions they reinforce the fear and insecurity which lead to social discord.

However, villains alone aren't to blame for this state of affairs. As *Civil War* shows, the foolish actions of several "heroes" are enough to vaporize a school. In this more subtle sense we can see how the state of nature exists even without "bad guys." It's not just the good or bad intentions of others that needs worrying about. It's the very fact that unrestrained and unpredictable power exists. You don't need super villains to make it a scary world: you just need uncertainty.

The Super Human Registration Act: Escaping the State of Nature

The collective horror over the Stamford incident makes the Marvel citizens question their trust in superheroes. They're scared, insecure, and vulnerable, and their response to this situation is extremely Hobbesian. For Hobbes, the only way to escape the state of nature is for individuals to collectively hand over their rights to a sovereign, who then rules over everyone. The idea is that by giving up their freedom and submitting to a single authority, everyone knows where they stand in relation to everyone else. People are no longer afraid of each other, because everyone is controlled by the same laws and can be expected to act in certain ways. There's no more uncertainty. There is only the sovereign and law.

You probably see where this is headed, but in case you read *Civil War* for the art, I'll explain. One of the repeated complaints in *Civil War* is that people no longer feel safe. They're tired of "Living in the Wild, Wild West," or "of having sixteen-year-olds drop buildings on them." These are arguments for security, yes, but also for predictability. People are scared because they don't know what to expect—will superheroes be professionals or kids in tights? Will they keep collateral damage to a minimum or will their good deeds destroy neighborhoods? The pro-registration camp argue that the only way to remove this fear is by making sure that people with extraordinary powers are trained and accountable, with government oversight. Supers agree to stop using their powers for their own agendas and follow a single authority. They give up their rights and submit to the Leviathan state.

For Hobbes, it was better to live in peace, even with no personal freedom at all, than to live in a constant state of fear and war. The pro-registration heroes are arguing a version of this—that it's better to give up individual freedom for the security of society than to preserve their independence. This is a Hobbesian solution to a Hobbesian problem, and it's a clear choice of safety over freedom. However, the question remains as to whether this "solution" is more dangerous than the disease it was meant to cure.

Hobbes: The First Mad (Political) Scientist

There's an interesting contrast between the two sides of the *Civil War* conflict. On the anti-registration side you find political idealists such as Patriot and Captain America, followed by moral barometers such as the Invisible Woman (Sue Storm) and Spider-Man. On the other, you find Tony Stark (technocrat-industrialist), Hank Pym (chemist and bio-geneticist) and Reed Richards (super genius). These three characters form the backbone of the pro-registration camp, and it's notable that they are all, in one form or another, scientists.

Why is this important? When Hobbes wrote, in addition to bloody war, the Scientific Revolution was in full swing across

Europe, and Hobbes witnessed the birth of modern science. In his lifetime, Galileo recorded the principle of inertia, the Royal Society was founded in England, and Newton derived the theory of gravity. These discoveries indicated that there were real, knowable laws that explained how the world worked. For Hobbes, this lead to the conviction that similar scientific principles existed for politics. This new "political science" when properly understood and applied would create a stable political order, and with it, peace.

Hobbes's conviction should seem familiar. We find a similar faith in scientific politics with Richards and Stark. Both men argue repeatedly for political strategy and order based on their own mathematic projections and scientific logic. The problem with their use of Hobbes's approach, however, is that Hobbes made two significant mistakes. Regarding the first, Sheldon Wolin writes:

> The first reaction of a modern reader to Hobbes's argument would be to point out that it rests upon a serious confusion of the methods of science with those of mathematics. Scientific method we regard as not being first and foremost a matter of logic and definition . . . science is primarily concerned with a method of experimentation which seeks empirical verification for its hypotheses. Geometry, which served as a model for Hobbes, does not purport to test its propositions by an appeal to experience, but rather on the consistent use of fixed definitions. (Sheldon Wolin, *Politics and Vision*, Princeton University Press, 1960, p. 224)

The reason that this is a political problem is that math, especially geometry, rests not on the observation of facts, but on deductive logic.

Deductive logic works by making successive claims based on the assumed truth of a starting principle—an example might look something like this:

1. **All men are mortal.**

2. **Spider-Man is a man.**

3. **Therefore, Spider-Man is mortal.**

In Hobbes, we start from the premise that the only way to escape the state of nature is to submit to the sovereign. Because we submit to be ruled, the sovereign is justified in ruling us. Therefore, the sovereign's laws are justified. This is more than tyrannical. It's also arbitrary. Whatever starting principle is chosen for ordering society, whether it be scientific truth, or another value such as beauty or justice, a deductive politics will arbitrarily enforce that standard—no matter which definition of "truth," "beauty," or "justice" you choose. It's from this arbitrariness that we can trace modern despotism to Hobbes. Consider Nazi Germany, which used a principle of ethnic supremacy to justify genocide, or Maoist China, which committed horrible atrocities in the name of modernization.

While "despotism" may seem like an extreme description of the superhero registration act, the connection applies. Most superheroes who join the pro-registration camp do so because "it's the law," though many doubt whether forcing supers to register is morally right. The confounding of "legality" and "moral correctness" is one of the perils of Hobbes's solution, and as readers of *Civil War* we are repeatedly asked whether it's enough to say that something is right simply because it is legal, or wrong because it's not. This reveals Hobbes's second faulty assumption: "that it was not only possible to reduce the political art to certain infallible rules, but that it was also desirable" (Wolin, *Politics and Vision*, p. 225).

Science versus Politics

You're probably asking if this is really fair. After all, Richards and Stark wouldn't be likely to confuse the methods of science with geometry as Hobbes did. They are modern scientists, and their approach would be based on modern scientific method instead of Hobbes's dangerous deductive "science." The question this raises, however, is whether Hobbes solution itself—a politics based on scientific models and laws, such as those which Richards and Stark use in *Civil War*—should worry us in it's own right.

There are several reasons to be wary of "scientific" politics. In the natural sciences, knowledge is gained through rigorous observation, theorizing, and experimentation. Scientific laws aim to describe the world as specifically as possible, and in such a way that we can predict and re-create certain phenomena. Because physics, chemistry, and biology are highly complex, experimentation involves the careful control and removal of random variables in order to isolate particular causal mechanisms. These methods run into several obstacles when carried over into the social sciences.

Since humans, unlike chemicals or atoms, are capable of making choices, there's the initial question of whether finding a "scientific law of human behavior" is even coherent. If we have free will, can't we simply defy any "behavioral law" we choose? There's an empirical problem here as well. Human behavior is affected by a variety of influences: culture, personal taste, religion, upbringing, even the biologic life cycle—yet the direct effect of these isn't necessarily observable. Observable human behavior doesn't reveal causes, but choices. To understand what *causes* individuals *to choose* requires a level of experimental control that usually demands a laboratory setting, and ethical issues aside (should we deliberately manipulate people in order to advance knowledge?) not many people act "normally" in labs. Without the ability to identify these causes, should we believe that anyone, even a genius like Richards, is capable of capturing human behavior with "scientific" certainty?

Even if we decide we aren't concerned with the *causes* of human behavior, just the behavior *itself*, we still run into problems. The language of the physical sciences, such as you might find in chemistry or physics, is mostly math. It makes sense to talk about speed, force, or size in terms of numbers and mathematic principles. In other words, a lot of what's studied in the physical sciences is quantifiable. It's a much different story with politics. Politics, after all, is concerned with people; not just how they interact, but also their values, what they consider good or bad, and how they collectively define themselves. These things don't exactly lend themselves to measurement. How do you accurately measure qualitative values like "happiness," or "justice"? Or for that matter, how do you quantify "freedom" and "security"?

Modern political science spends a lot of time trying to do exactly this, and it wouldn't be fair to say that quantification is inherently bad—it's not. We can and do learn quite a bit by observing and studying our own choices and patterns of behavior. The trouble with applying the quantitative approach of the hard sciences to politics isn't simply that it forces values onto dubious scales, it's that things which can't be measured have a tendency to be dismissed as unimportant. Austrian thinker Friedrich Hayek puts it clearly:

> We know, of course . . . a great many facts which we cannot measure and on which indeed we have only some very imprecise and general information. And because of the effects of these facts in any particular instance cannot be confirmed by quantitative evidence, they are sim-

ply disregarded by those sworn to admit only what they regard as scientific evidence: they thereupon happily proceed on the fiction that the factors which they can measure are the only ones that are relevant. ("The Pretense of Knowledge," in *New Studies in Philosophy, Economics, and the History of Ideas*, University of Chicago Press, 1985, p. 28)

The trouble with limiting yourself to studying only what is quantifiable is that you can't take into account those things that experience, or even common sense, might tell you are important. And in politics, where outcomes affect human lives, ignoring what's important can have terrible costs.

The Death of Goliath

There's a great scene in *Civil War* between Sue Storm and her husband, Dr. Reed Richards. He's engrossed in his work, and when Sue asks why he isn't upset about half of their Christmas-card list getting carted off to jail, he points at lines of mathematical equations on the walls as explanation. "What are you talking about?" she responds. "That's just gobbledygook."[1]

Sue's inability to understand Richards's explanation demonstrates the problem of scientific reasoning in political decision making. As a public activity involving many different opinions and considerations, politics requires communication. The specialized knowledge and mathematical phrasing of science can make it very difficult to understand from the outside; but it can also make it hard for the scientist, thinking in a very logical and mathematical way, to communicate or even understand the consequences of her actions in political terms. Consider, for instance, the case of the atomic bomb. Political theorist Hannah Arendt comments:

> The reason why it may be wise to distrust the political judgment of scientists *qua* scientists is not primarily their lack of "character"—that they did not refuse to develop atomic weapons—or their naïveté—that they did not understand that once these weapons were developed they would be the last to be consulted about their use—but precisely the fact that they move in a world where speech has lost its power . . .

---

[1] Mark Millar (w), Steve McNiven (p), Dexter Vines et al (i), Morry Hollowell (c), "Civil War" *Civil War* #2 (Marvel Comics, 2006), p. 6/1.

> There may be truths beyond speech, and they may be of great rele-
> vance to man in the singular, that is, to man in so far as he is not a
> political being . . . Men in the plural . . . can experience meaningful-
> ness only because they can talk with and make sense to each other
> and to themselves. (*The Human Condition*, University of Chicago
> Press, 1958, p. 4)

The A-bomb moment in *Civil War* is the death of Goliath. This is
when both sides realize what's at stake, and some heroes begin to
have second thoughts about their choices. Goliath is killed by a
clone of Thor—a former superhero and Norse god—which is created by Richards and Stark as a weapon. The clone is controlled by
a mind chip that forces him to act within the confines of the law,
which he does, even while shooting a column of lightning through
Goliath's heart.

In the fallout from this event, characters repeatedly ask what
went wrong. The simple assumption was that the clone would act
the same as the true Thor, complete with the ability to exercise
restraint. The episode shows Pym, Stark, and Richards's blind faith in
their approach, but also a similar blindness in the other superheroes.
The shock of Goliath's death depicts how poorly some heroes understood that the absolute claims of a scientific approach would be
insensitive to shifting human categories such as friend or foe.

Importantly, Goliath's death is justified by the pro-registration
camp because he was breaking a law that would "protect people's
lives." The means-end reasoning seen here is also apparent in the
construction of "42," a new, secret high-tech prison. The justification
for 42 is clear: the only way to ensure that all supers in society are
registered is to remove those who refuse. Since supers could escape
from a regular prison, 42 has to be located in the Negative Zone—
a place literally outside of the world. However, it's not just villains
who get sent to 42, but *any* person with super powers who refuses
to register—whether they're engaged in public "heroics" or not. If
the very presence of super powers constitutes a risk, anything less
than complete submission of the super population would be insuf-
ficient for a secure society. This illustrates the problem: a scientific
approach may tell you exactly how to solve a political crisis, but it
can't tell you when the price of that solution is too high.

Surprisingly, it's a villain who points this out in the clearest
terms. Thinker, a genius in his own right—mocks Richards after
seeing his walls of scribbled social projections:

I see no flaws in your equations. The science is unassailable . . . And you. So brilliant, yet so naïve. You thought you could make these moves without personal cost, without doing evil yourself . . . understanding every intricacy of the big picture, while blindly walking further and further down the path of evil.[2]

Science is not inherently immoral; it's simply not really concerned with morality. Whether science is *used* in a moral way or not depends on the people who exercise the knowledge it provides. Expecting science to provide only answers that are morally good, just because the question asked was well intended, is to make a potentially terrible mistake.

Whose Side Are You On?

In the final pages of *Civil War*, Tony Stark leads the mother of one of the Stamford Elementary victims through the S.H.I.E.L.D. helicarrier. He tells her about a list of one hundred things that he, Pym, and Richards have put together to improve the world. Number 42 on that list—the high-tech prison—has been met with public approval, and with the surrender of Captain America's resistance the war over the registration act has finished. Stark ends the narrative with a smile and a vision: "The best is yet to come, sweetheart. That's a promise."[3]

This is an ending Hobbes would appreciate. Without the fear of superheroes toppling buildings or stepping on cars, people can get on with the important business of leading their lives. Stark is the new head of S.H.I.E.L.D., and promises to benevolently oversee the actions of his peers. The public has superheroes they can believe in again. Everyone is finally safe under the law.

What I've hopefully shown, however, is that making the trade-off between safety and freedom in the way the Marvel characters choose to isn't as simple as picking between two equally good options. Rather, it's making the choice between two kinds of risk. We can accept the uncertainty that comes with living in a free

[2] J. Michael Stracyznski and Dwayne McDuffie (w), M. Mckone (p), Andy Lanning et al. (i), Paul Mounts (c), "Civil War" *Fantastic Four* #542 (Marvel Comics, 2007), pp. 21/2–3.

[3] Mark Millar (w), Steve McNiven (p), Dexter Vines et al (i), Morry Hollowell (c), "Civil War" *Civil War* # 7 (Marvel Comics, 2006), p. 23/2.

world, and risk that the people around us may exercise their freedom in ways that put us in danger. Or we can choose to give up our freedom to be more secure, and risk that the individuals we trust with our safety will make poor decisions—even *if* they're for the right reasons.

Stark's closing promise of a better world isn't meant insincerely, nor should it be seen as impossible. Political thinkers stretching back to Plato have imagined communities where order forms the basis for ideal society, but these societies are rarely "free" in the way we think of the word. It's also worth remembering the costs of Stark's "better world." The Hobbesian project and its corresponding faith in the scientific direction of politics, which lies at the heart of the registration act and the approach adopted by Stark, Richards, and Pym leads heroes to accept the imprisonment of friends, the disintegration of personal relationships, and the death of a good man. Is this price too high? Is it better to be free, or is it better to be safe?

Whose side are you on?

11

Who Trusts the Watchmen?

RAFAELA HILLERBRAND and
ANDERS SANDBURG

EDITOR'S NOTE: *On the off chance you haven't read* Watchmen *or seen the recent movie, you should be warned that this essay contains major spoilers because the coolest and most thought-provoking stuff happens at the end.*

> I did the right thing, didn't I?
> —The World's Smartest Man

In an alternate 1985 where the United States won the Vietnam war, Nixon is still president, and fast-food comes from Gunga Diner, the US is edging closer to a nuclear war with the Soviet Union. As the diplomatic situation deteriorates, Rorschach and Nite Owl uncover a terrifying conspiracy.

Adrien Veidt, the world-famous one-time costumed crime fighter Ozymandias, has secretly orchestrated a series of murders and other crimes as part of some larger and more mysterious design. Rorschach and Nite Owl confront Veidt in his luxurious Antarctic headquarters, and like every other comic-book supervillain, Veidt explains the details of his plan. He recognized that crime and corruption were just symptoms of an underlying social problem that no amount of bare-knuckle justice could resolve. Accordingly, he set his sights higher and turned his prodigious intellect to the most pressing social problem: the nuclear arms race between the United States and the Soviet Union. Concluding that it would inevitably end in a nuclear war annihilating mankind, Veidt explains to his Anarctic visitors that

"End of the world" does the concept no justice. The world's present would end. Its future, immeasurably vaster, would also vanish. Even our past would be cancelled. Our struggle from the primal ooze, every childbirth, every personal sacrifice rendered meaningless, leading only to dust, tossed on the void-winds.

Leaving his cape and mask behind, Veidt set up a complex and long-term plan. He became a philanthropist businessman, invested in new technologies, removed unpredictable people, and set in motion a scheme to teleport a monstrous telepathic lifeform of his own creation into the heart of New York City. (The film version detonates an experimental power plant based on Dr. Manhattan's energy source.) The creature's death on arrival will kill three million New Yorkers and psychologically scar millions more. A shocked world will believe in a dreadful alien threat that must be repelled, and the world's political superpowers will unite against a common threat, all former enmities aside.

It's truly a breathtaking plan, and it would be the cliché in the last act of every comic book we've ever read except that Adrian Veidt unleashes it thirty minutes before Rorschach and Nite-Owl arrive. Veidt kills three million New Yorkers, the United States and Soviet Union draw back from the brink of nuclear war, and Rorschach and Nite Owl watch helplessly as their efforts to bring the Comedian's killer to justice are dwarfed by larger events. Veidt will get away with it too. Exposing him would undo the peace purchased with millions of lives, and so all but one of the remaining adventurers agree to keep the truth a secret.

"Not even in the face of Armageddon," says Rorschach. Though he offers no further reasoning than "evil must be punished," his break with Ozymandias, Nite-Owl, Silk Spectre, and Dr. Manhattan highlights a special problem at the intersection of morality and power. It was a problem known to the Roman satirist Juvenal when he asked, *quis custodiet ipsos custodes*, or "who watches the watchmen?" (Juvenal's original passage directly refers to the difficulty of keeping an adulterous wife under guard at home, for the wife in turn seduces the guards as well! But the quotation is most often applied to political life.) When society grants to a few the power to protect the many, how will the many in turn protect themselves against the few?

The problem survives Juvenal to this day, and imagine how much more pressing it would be in a world where the protectors are self-appointed, anonymous, and extremely powerful. The alternate ending in *Watchmen*'s screen version suggests that it may not even be possible for society to protect itself against its self-appointed protectors. If so, then whether society embraces its protectors—be they street-sweeping ciphers like Rorschach or cosmically-powerful entities like Dr. Manhattan—depends on what they can be trusted to do. Answering that question means knowing something about the moral perspectives that drive them.

Clashing Moralities

Why can't Rorschach simply accept that the New Yorkers killed by Veidt's designer alien are already lost? For Rorschach, wrong actions remain wrong even if they avert a greater evil. Thus, Veidt's killing of millions can never be justified, not even if it saves the whole of the rest of the human race. Philosophers refer to this kind of moral reasoning as *deontological ethics* from the Greek word for duty (*deon*).

The most famous deontological ethical system was formulated by Immanuel Kant. Kant would probably not have approved of Rorschach, but he would have agreed that some duties can never be compromised. Kant governed all actions by a principle he called the *categorical imperative*, which he thought must be respected by all rational beings. In the *Metaphysics of Morals*, he formulated the categorical imperative in this way:

> Act only according to that maxim whereby you can at the same time will that it should become a universal law. (*Grounding for the Metaphysics of Morals*, Hackett, p 30)[1]

Deontological ethics seem to square most people's powerful moral intuitions about prohibitions on murder or rape, and with religious ethics so far as sacred duties are concerned. Are there things you must *never* do? Rorschach was born when he discovered the grisly murder of little Blair Roche, and he entertained no doubts about the answer to that question. If you don't either, then you also have some deontological intuitions.

---

[1] Kant had several formulations of the Categorical Imperative, all of which he thought were equivalent to one another. See Chapter 5 in this volume for a different formulation.

By contrast, Adrian Veidt would reject unconditional duties. As the smartest man in the world, he not only sees the approaching nuclear holocaust, but he also thinks he sees a way out of it, so he does what Rorschach would never do. Rorschach could never endorse killing three million people, even if it meant saving every human being on the planet, and the same is true for Kant because he recognizes a distinction between doing and allowing. According to Kant, doing something wrong is worse than allowing something bad to happen by failing to act. For both Kant and Rorschach, killing three million people can never be justified because life has an absolute value that cannot be quantified or traded. Adrian Veidt's hands are wet with the blood of three million people, but who would have been to blame if humanity had annihilated itself? Not Rorschach, his hands would have been clean of innocent blood, and that makes all the difference in the world.

Somebody Has to Save the World

Numbers matter to Adrian Veidt. His ethical convictions form the counterpoint to Rorschach's deontology. For Veidt, only the final outcome matters. He's convinced that the world is approaching a nuclear holocaust that possibly signifies the end of all human life on Earth, so he believes he must do everything in his power to prevent this from happening—even if it costs three million lives.

Veidt's moral analysis is simply *utilitarian*, which means that what is morally correct is what benefits the most people. Utilitarian philosophers such as Jeremy Bentham, John Stuart Mill, and Henry Sidgwick have expressed the principle in terms of promoting "the greatest happiness for the greatest number."[2] Today, utilitarian analysis frequently provides the framework for many kinds of public policy from healthcare to climate change impact to the risks of new technologies. Isn't public policy *supposed* to maximize benefits to the public? To the extent that you agree, you're probably motivated by some kind of utilitarian intuition.

Veidt wants to reduce the total amount of suffering in the world, and what he does could be called proactive sabotage. If nuclear

---

[2] This principle was first formulated by Jeremy Bentham in *An Introduction to the Principles of Morals and Legislation* (1789). For more about utilitarianism, see Chapters 8 and 12 in this volume.

war would annihilate all value mankind has ever achieved or will achieve, then the least harmful action that prevents nuclear war is what Veidt must do. Note that Veidt's utilitarianism rejects the moral distinction between doing and allowing that Kant embraced. So even if Veidt has the blood of three million innocents on his hands, unlike Rorschach, he would see humanity's annihilation as part of his responsibility as well. After all, didn't he have the power to do something about it? Doesn't great responsibility come with great power?

Maybe so, but if what justifies an act is its outcome, that can leave one in a difficult position at the moment of decision. Veidt is the world's smartest man, but even he failed to anticipate that Rorschach would mail his journal to the *New Frontiersman*. It is unclear whether the journalist Seymour will read it and *see more* than he is supposed to see, though the screen version seems to lean towards his doing so. If he does, the publication of Rorschach's journal would unravel Veidt's plan and render the deaths of millions of New Yorkers in vain.

That said, doesn't Adrian have an ace in the hole so far as the future is concerned? Dr. Manhattan seems willing to go along with Veidt's plan and appears persuaded by Veidt's utilitarian arguments. Dr. Manhattan is so convinced that even with his newfound respect for life, he is willing to kill Rorschach to protect Ozymandias's secret. When someone who can read the future sides with the World's Smartest Man, isn't that good reason to think that numbers will come out right?

The Demon-Haunted Superheroes

Alan Moore is not the first person to imagine a superhuman intelligence that knows all the details and can predict all the consequences of every event. In 1814, the French mathematician Pierre-Simon Laplace invented a thought experiment philosophers refer to as Laplace's Demon. Laplace's Demon knows all the laws of nature and where all particles are at a certain instant. He can calculate exactly how they will move far into the future. In *Watchmen*, Dr. Manhattan seems to be such a creature, so why doesn't his complicity with Veidt settle the question of utilitarian outcomes?

Because Dr. Manhattan has a physical brain, in most cases it will take him almost as a long to make predictions as the systems needs to achieve the actual state. This is because the only way to account for all of reality's enormously complex variables is to model it in its entirety—every particle and every state change in every combination. The irony is that if Dr. Manhattan *really* wanted to know the future, then even with all his powers running overtime, he'd have to wait for it to happen like everyone else. Thus, his finding would come too late.

Furthermore, because he himself is part of the system, then electrons and other particles will change in his brain while he processes predictions. These changes will change the state of the system as a whole so that predictions take even longer. This self-referential problem ultimately means that Ozymandias's tachyon satellites prove just as unnecessary as his attempt to remove Dr. Manhattan's intrinsic field.

Nonetheless, within a more limited predictive horizon, Dr. Manhattan might be more successful, and he often seems highly aware of this. In the book's closing panels, he cannot reassure Veidt about the outcome of his plan because utilitarian judgments are based on final outcomes. The problem as he puts it is that "nothing ends, Adrian. Nothing ever ends." Even as a stand-in for Laplace's Demon, Dr. Manhattan would ultimately be unable to settle whether Veidt's action could be justified by his own utilitarian reasoning.

Even so, Dr. Manhattan does go along with the plan. Many contemporary utilitarians hold that it's enough to reason from the *foreseeable* consequences of an action instead of its *actual* consequences when making moral assessments. Veidt might find that reassuring, but he probably shouldn't, given the scale of his actions. After all, would you hold blameless someone who needlessly killed millions because he wasn't more able to predict the outcomes of his actions? Why then does Dr. Manhattan go along with him?

Beyond Moral?

One answer is that Dr. Manhattan goes along with everyone and everything. Throughout the story, he is enigmatically passive and acts only when acted on by others. Whether it's Adrian Veidt, the United States government, or Laurie Juspeczyck on Mars, Dr. Manhattan's amazing powers apparently don't include the ability to say no. Though he seems well aware of his predictive limits, his preference for the role of the neutral observer is probably not the reason he remains so passive.

Dr. Manhattan is as remote from morality as he is from everything else about his humanity. As with the Comedian, morality seems arbitrary to him, and so he takes a fairly passive standpoint for most of the book. "Other people seem to make all my moves for me," he muses. In a sense, he is much like the natural forces at his command: he is frequently inscrutable and completely unmotivated by what he sees as arbitrary moral demands. But is there no moral perspective that makes sense of Dr. Manhattan?

In fact there are two. The first is nihilism, the view that there is no such thing as morality.[3] Perhaps Dr. Manhattan behaves like a force of nature because he has no basis for embracing moral values. Whatever else moral values are, they are not empirical properties like mass or charge, and so they remain mysterious to him if they are not merely arbitrary. Even when persuaded to save humanity, Dr. Manhattan's interest in human life is merely an interest in the value of its rarity as a "thermodynamic miracle."

Dr. Manhattan may be a kind of moral nihilist, but perhaps we can see him in another light as well. Arthur Schopenhauer (1788–1860) was a German philosopher influenced by Buddhist and Indian ideas, and he argued that the only response to the evil of the world is a life that abstains from all its pains and pleasures. Accordingly, he thought that the best life was a self-contained life. Perhaps Dr. Manhattan would agree with Schopenhauer that correct moral action, regardless of one's ethical system, is impossible. If so, he might act on utilitarian grounds to the extent that he remains interested in thermodynamic rarities. However, when that interest waned, Dr. Manhattan's decision to ultimately leave Earth and humanity behind would make perfect sense as a kind of principled withdrawal.

This Must Be How Ordinary People Feel

Now we can revisit Juvenal's question, and ask with him, "Who watches the watchmen?" Remember that this is a question about trust. Because there is no final assurance that society's protectors—the Watchmen—*will* protect society, all that is left is the extent to

---

[3] For more on moral nihilism, see Chaper 7 in this volume.

which we trust our own predictions about their behavior. In the empirical sciences, trust of this kind is relatively straightforward. A theory that makes predictions about future events can be checked against reality. If those predictions are correct, you trust the theory. However, in the case of human behavior, predictive success with respect to people's actions is more difficult. In empirical measures, what is trust's mass, and what is the vector and velocity of moral outrage?

For such things there are no scientific instruments, and the best predictors of human behavior remain the value systems to which people appeal in the explanation of their actions. As an individual you trust your partner if you believe that he or she shares the value of fidelity that prohibits affairs. As a member of society, you can only trust society's guardians if you believe they will act on shared social values.

What counts as a shared social value can be contentious, but there do seem to be some clear cases. One example might be the Golden Rule of doing to others what you would have them do to you. This is a value shared by many cultural traditions, but there are others. The point here is not to come up with a list of what could count as a shared social value, but merely to show that there are such values, and that even if some might be controversial, there are probably others that are not.

So whom can we trust?

We can start with Dr. Manhattan, but mainly to set him aside. He is clearly beyond human community and the values human communities share, so he makes a poor candidate for trust. When combined with his immense power, we can imagine all kinds of moral catastrophe to which Dr. Manhattan would be entirely indifferent. (The alternate ending in the filmed version of *Watchmen* suggests this possibility quite starkly.) It seems pretty difficult to imagine Dr. Manhattan's moral indifference inspiring the kind of trust we invest in society's protectors, so he is probably a poor candidate for that job.

What about Rorschach? His absolute unwillingness to compromise seems like a good trait when he's talking about the deaths of three million New Yorkers, but like his namesake, Rorschach's morality is not unblemished. He acquires information by injuring random people in seedy bars and other bad parts of town. He assumes that his prospective informants are all scum and deserve it somehow, even if they're not culpable for the crimes he happens to be pursuing at the moment. Though Rorschach won't compromise to protect Adrian Veidt's secret, it also looks like his violence isn't sensitive to any conception of justice but his own. In short, the extent to which you can trust Rorschach is exactly the extent to which *you* happen to agree with *his* values, rather than the other way around. This is hardly going to reassure the members of society under his protection because they'll finally realize that that category is vanishingly small!

And what of Adrian Veidt? The World's Smartest Man seems guided by utilitarian thinking. Clearly, Veidt acts from good motives, but his moral reasoning brings him to murder millions of New Yorkers in pursuit of his cause. Making matters worse, this apocalyptic act may have been in vain if the journalist from the *New Frontiersman* reads Rorschach's journal—a possibility the movie suggests more strongly than the book. Veidt is smart, but he is nonetheless fallible. The World's Smartest Man fails to kill Dr. Manhattan, vainly kills his beloved pet in the attempt, exhibits genuine surprise when his plan finally succeeds, and finally wonders whether he did the right thing. These are hardly the actions of an infallible genius, and what do we finally say about a man who's willing to take on such risky projects with millions of lives hanging in the balance? Maybe he's not some "Republic serial villain," but Veidt is still a paradigm example of what this book is all about.

In the end—Dr. Manhattan's cryptic denial notwithstanding—*Watchmen* is a story about the moral and intellectual fallibility that's part of everyone's experience. So answering Juvenal's question perhaps means first answering the question Nite Owl asks rhetorically as he wrestles with the decision to keep Veidt's secret: "how can humans make decisions like this?" How indeed! But to the extent that any protector of society recognizes such limits on their own moral and intellectual powers, we as a society might finally have the beginnings of a rational trust in the watchmen's ability to keep a just watch. We can perhaps trust that where our protectors have clear knowledge of their limits, they will likewise limit their interventions on our behalf to those actions that the barest necessities of protection require.

12

New Wars,
New Boundaries

JOHN OSTRANDER

The following is an interview between Jennifer Ludlum, the newly appointed liaison between the White House and the National Security Council, and Walker Smith, co-ordinator of Metahuman Covert Operations for the NSC, as part of an overall evaluation of governmental sponsored metahuman projects. At this session, the topic was Amanda Waller, creator and head of Task Force X, colloquially known as the Suicide Squad.

JENNIFER LUDLUM: We now come to the so-called Suicide Squad. It's represented to be an American Covert Actions group that uses metahuman felons—supervillains—as operatives on missions deemed to be in the American interest, is that right?

WALKER SMITH: The concept dates back at least to the Second World War where non metahuman prisoners in the military volunteered for hazardous duty in what became dubbed the "Suicide Squadron". These days, the operatives are all metahuman criminals—"supervillains"—who are convicted felons currently serving time. Their prison terms are mitigated for successful completion—and survival—of the selected missions by the metahuman operatives.

LUDLUM: How did Amanda Waller become involved?

SMITH: Mrs. Waller came from the projects in Chicago where she saw both her daughter and her husband killed by gangs. She determined to get the rest of her family out of the projects and managed to get them all off to colleges, after which she herself attended and graduated from college. She became the campaign manager for Marvin Collins, helping him win his Congressional seat. In

Washington as Collin's aide and while researching a different project, she came across a description of the earlier Suicide Squadron, Waller saw possibilities for it in the modern world using supervillains.

LUDLUM: The Squad is a covert action group?

SMITH: Originally, the existence of the Squad was not known to the general public. The United States government had complete deniability as to their actions. Even after their cover was blown, the Squad was still active.

LUDLUM: Tell me about Waller.

SMITH: Mrs. Waller is a formidable personality. She's nicknamed "The Wall"—a name she seems to like. She's aggressive, confrontational, and known for a no-holds-barred approach. She can also be surprisingly thoughtful.

LUDLUM: The missions the Squad undertakes are possibly illegal and highly dangerous. Have there been fatalities?

SMITH: Of course. Part of the reason for using the metahuman criminals is that they are more expendable.

LUDLUM: The Squad also has non-criminals going on the missions as well.

SMITH: Yes. They need to ride herd on the bad guys. A version of the Squad—with which Mrs. Waller was not involved—tried using only villains. It was a total disaster.

LUDLUM: She also has other means for ensuring co-operation.

SMITH: Yes. Originally there was a sort of bracelet which could blow the felon's arm off if they tried to escape or otherwise sabotage the mission. These days they install a chip in the base of the skull that can blow the back of the felon's head off.

LUDLUM: Mrs. Waller has had occasion to use these devices?

SMITH: Yes. She doesn't have to use it often. The message gets out—they're not playing around.

LUDLUM: is that legal?

SMITH: It's within Mrs. Waller's authority. The only cases where it was used was a prison riot where guards' lives were at risks and on missions where the safety of the other team members were jeopardized, where the mission has been put at risk by the offending operative, or the operative is trying to renege on the agreement or betray both the mission and their team members. These are combat situations and different rules apply.

LUDLUM: Who picks the missions?

SMITH: That's usually done in Washington. Mrs. Waller has input—lots of input. She's been known to initiate a mission on her own when circumstances demanded it.

LUDLUM: Do these missions ever bother Mrs. Waller—or you?

SMITH: They've got to be done. The Squad's first mission, for example, involved a terrorist-for-hire group that called itself the Jihad. Sponsored by a rogue state. Mrs. Waller had an operative inside the Jihad and she knew that the Jihad were practicing to launch an attack on a United States airport as Air Force One was going to arrive and kill the President as well as many civilians. The Squad struck first. They hit the Jihad in their own headquarters and killed most of them. The Jihad later reformed and attacked New York City, proving the justification for the Squad's earlier attack. Again, we intercepted them and killed as many of them as we could.

LUDLUM: So the end justifies the means?

SMITH: If it's outcomes that matter, then yes, whatever it takes.

LUDLUM: We've heard that kind of sophistry before.

SMITH: I'm more utilitarian than sophist if I remember my philosophy courses from college.

LUDLUM: So the moral justification for your actions is that the consequences will produce a greater good?

SMITH: The Squad's actions mean greater safety for the citizens of this country and, ultimately, for the world. They mean less danger to their lives, and more freedom to choose the life they like. The hard reality of democratic politics is that politicians who keep their seats are going to court the approval of the greatest possible number of constituents, and those constituents in turn measure political job performance by the quality of their own lives. The greatest happiness or well-being for the greatest number of people isn't sophistry.

LUDLUM: But we're asking about the well-being of Mrs. Waller's agents too. *If* they survive duty on her "Suicide Squad," don't they just return for more jail time?

SMITH: For the most part, she's dealing with a lot of scum and thugs here. They're in prison as the *consequence* of their actions which are usually pretty nasty. They also have the *choice* of being on the Squad and going on the mission. Once they do that, they live by her rules or they live with her consequences.

LUDLUM: So you don't regard them as having any natural rights or *intrinsic* worth?

SMITH: The Declaration of Independence and the United States Constitution recognize natural rights, but they also recognize that people can forfeit them. The felons who work for the Squad threw away their rights when they committed the crimes for which they were duly tried, found guilty, and slapped into prison.

LUDLUM: So you do accept that some things have an intrinsic worth?

SMITH: No, and I doubt Mrs. Waller does either but we didn't write the Constitution. Jeremy Bentham once said that natural rights are "nonsense on stilts." They're a legal fiction in the same way that a corporation as a person is a legal fiction. We all are born with the right to life, liberty, and the pursuit of happiness, among others. That's how the Declaration puts it, but if that's so, they don't do any work in the real world. Lincoln and Roosevelt suspended certain civil rights when they thought they had to, but individual citizens have no more of a natural right to rule themselves than Britain's monarchy had to rule us during the Revolution. That's why the Declaration of Independence was such a radical document; it rejected the idea that the right to rule was embodied in the King or Queen and the aristocracy. The Declaration may have turned that upside down, but that doesn't mean the idea of natural rights suddently made any more sense.

LUDLUM: So if your legal authority is backed by the Constitution, but your moral justification is utilitarian, then how do you and Mrs. Waller reconcile the two?

SMITH: Unlike the Declaration, the Constitution is a pragmatic document. This is the preamble of the Constitution, the whole thing: "We the People of the United States, *in Order to form a more perfect Union*, establish Justice, insure domestic Tranquility, provide for the common defense, promote the general Welfare, and secure the Blessings of Liberty to ourselves and our Posterity, do ordain and establish this Constitution for the United States of America." The Constitution is a contract we entered into to achieve a certain good. We did it because we *wanted* the goods we thought it would get us, not because we couldn't have done anything else.

LUDLUM: I think your job is making you cynical.

SMITH: Government is *always* pragmatic which means it's almost always utilitarian. It fails when it tries to be anything else. You want sophistry? Sophistry is Chief Justice Taney of the United States Supreme Court dismissing Dred Scott's antebellum lawsuit to gain his freedom on the grounds that slaves had no standing to bring a lawsuit. What ideals made seven of the court's nine justice decide that negroes didn't have the same human rights that white people had? We didn't settle that question with a war of words and abstractions, and in the end it was people like me that *made* America's five million slaves equal.

LUDLUM: So you want to be a pragmatist? Fine, let's return to the practical details of the Squad—your missions are covert.

SMITH: They start that way. They don't always end that way.

LUDLUM: They usually involve violating the borders of other countries to commit illegal activities including but not limited to kidnapping, theft, and assassination.

SMITH: Sounds nasty when you put it like that but—yes.

LUDLUM: And you would justify these acts as moral?

SMITH: Morally necessary. Hasn't the Squad saved thousands of lives for the ones that they take? Aren't the lives that they save those of non-combatants and innocent civilians in our country and in the country involved? Terrorists groups regularly locate their headquarters amid civilian populations or next to a hospital. They use the civilian population as human shields. An air strike can cause many innocent dead and wounded, but the Squad can be inserted, hit the target, accomplish the mission, and do so with little or no civilian casualties.

LUDLUM: That would be true in wartime, but most of your missions occur without war being declared. Does Mrs. Waller's authority, in your opinion, include the right to declare war on America's enemies?

SMITH: Come on. Congress hasn't actually issued a formal declaration of war since World War II, but that hasn't stopped our government from exercising force when it thought it was justified in doing so.

LUDLUM: And I suppose you think you and Mrs. Waller are justified in doing so?

SMITH: At least we recognize parameters for restraint. People throw around terms like "just war" or "war crimes" without thinking very much about what that means. The Western just war tradition probably started with St. Augustine as the Roman empire was falling down around his ears. Latin Christians for the first time fought other Christians as converted Visigoths and other Germanic tribes swept into the falling empire on the heels of Rome's withdrawing legions. Killing in war is one thing, but killing fellow Christians is something else, so Augustine distinguished between the political decision to start a war and the moral conduct of the men fighting it. He was of the opinion that those who obeyed orders were like a sword being wielded and thus, could not be held responsible for the decision to commence hostilities. It could be argued we're just weapons too, but after the trial of the Nazis at Nuremburg, the world doesn't much care for the answer, "I was only following orders." So yes, Mrs. Waller has a responsibility to justify both the decision to deploy and the conduct of the Squad in the field. We need to be aware of what the mission is going to do, and since most of the metahumans we work with either don't know or don't care about the consequences of what they do, the burden of their conduct has falls on us as well.

LUDLUM: How can you think the actions of people like Deadshot or the General or Captain Boomerang are defensible? These are people—thugs, remember—who have never been indoctrinated in the Uniform Code of Military Justice.

SMITH: The Squad uses nasty people to do nasty things. That's *why* Mrs. Waller uses them. They're going to behave as they behave and we know that going in. That's also the reason for the good guys who go along on the mission—let's call them the shepherds to the black sheep. They make certain that the mission gets completed and none of our little flock goes wandering, but they also keep them reined in.

LUDLUM: So Mrs. Waller is a commander who vouches for her troops, but that's only one side of the moral question. Should the Squad be engaging in paramilitary activities on foreign soil at all? If the acts themselves are illegal and immoral, are you no better than those you attack?

SMITH: The Squad's actions are defensible under the same standards that justify conventional military forces everywhere else in the civilized world. If military action is never justified, then fine, but we acknowledge a moral *necessity* to both defend our way of life and to limit the harms of war. Striking that balance is hard, but the difference between us and them are those limiting principles. Just wars require *just cause* to engage in acts that in and of themselves are usually pretty heinous. Just wars are declared by *proper authority*; usually means a state that itself has a proper relationship between itself and its people. Just war means having *right intent*— the purpose is not just a land grab or a convenient political end, but for justice or something. A just war has a *reasonable chance for success*. Can you do what you set out to do? What will it cost in human life and national resources? Maybe most importantly, just wars have aims proportional to the justice of their causes, and that's maybe where the Squad distinguishes itself. You want to depose Black Adam in Khandaq? How about taking down rogue terrorist factions on foreign soil? The Squad can *do* that without committing the United States to a large-scale, protracted conflict that costs twelve times my annual budget.

LUDLUM: Those are nice distinctions, but you haven't answered the question. Are you using the Squad to fight a war?

SMITH: None of our opponents are related in any way, so I would characterize it as a series of small nasty wars. The common denominator would be a perceived threat to the citizens of the United States or to United States government interests.

LUDLUM: There's a difference between those two. One could question whether the latter represents just cause, or whether it's an ill-defined term—a catch-all for illegitimate activities.

SMITH: As well as some legitimate ones, but you're off-point. An attack on the people *or* the government is an attack on the United States, period. You're confusing just cause with the separate condition that war must be declared by *proper authority*.

LUDLUM: And that's your authority?

SMITH: That's the United States government's authority. As I said, Mrs. Waller doesn't determine the missions although she does have a voice in that selection. The selection is done by *authorized* people within the U.S. government, including the office of the President—which included your predecessor—Congressional leaders working on select committees, and members of various agencies and the military.

LUDLUM: Determined in secret.

SMITH: It *is* a covert operations group.

LUDLUM: So the United States government can legitimately declare war when it determines that just cause has been met in its own case, and it does this with no oversight? Pardon me, sir, but I can't imagine you're that naïve.

SMITH: You probably can't imagine a lot of things about what we do, but that's why we're here isn't it? Let's cut to the chase. Do our missions have a *reasonable chance for success*? Despite our code name, yes, they usually do. We are willing to sacrifice lives but we don't throw them away because that would make it hard to get new recruits among the metahuman criminal population. Are our actions *proportional* to the mission requirements? Yes, but given the kind of missions we run, that sometimes means we leave the target pretty messy.

LUDLUM: But that's just the point. The missions you run are no different than—

SMITH: The Squad's missions are a classic example of *right intent*. Every government has a right to protect itself, and there's no virtue in waiting for a bloody nose when the other guy is swinging his fist. What we don't do is grab land, assassinate foreign leaders, or enslave ethnic populations.

LUDLUM: But your own utilitarian philosophy requires you to do whatever is most expedient for the greater good, but now you're telling us that you observe strictly principled limits. So which is it, are your missions motivated by conscience or political expediency?

SMITH: No mission is wholly motivated by one or the other.

LUDLUM: But they are more one than the other, aren't they?

SMITH: Yes. A few—very few—have wound up being more about politics and policy than doing what was necessary, what was right.

LUDLUM: Mrs. Waller went ahead with them anyway.

SMITH: She made her objections known. The decision was made to go forward. The only alternative would have been for her to resign her position in protest.

LUDLUM: Arguably, that would have been the right thing to do.

SMITH: The mission would have gone forward on any case and she would have been replaced—most likely by someone who would not object in the future and who would have failed at the job.

LUDLUM: You don't know that.

SMITH: She wasn't going to risk it.

LUDLUM: So Mrs. Waller went ahead with something she knew or believed to be morally or ethically wrong.

SMITH: Yes.

LUDLUM: Mr. Smith, when it comes right down to it, what separates you or Mrs. Waller from the metahuman criminals you use as operatives?

SMITH: Again, *right intent*. Most of the Squad's members are interested in money or power or revenge, but we have to take the high road.

LUDLUM: There are those who say it's about personal power with Mrs. Waller too . . .

SMITH: Then they don't know her. She's not shy about getting or using power, I admit, especially political power, but it is always in service of getting the job done. One of her daughters was raped and killed and her husband died seeking to avenge her. It was a grand gesture, but it didn't bring her daughter back and her husband's death left Mrs. Waller and the rest of their children very vulnerable. These days she tries to anticipate a problem. She sees it coming and stops it before it hurts or kills others. She does whatever it takes because the stakes are literally life and death. I do not pretend Mrs. Waller is a nice person or maybe even a good one but she *is* making a moral choice. She stands by the consequences of her acts and is willing to be judged by them. Which is more than most politicians seem willing to do.

LUDLUM: Even if those consequences include the deaths of innocents caught between the Squad and its targets?

SMITH: When there were set battles with a recognizable foe, nations fought ordinary wars—if there is such a thing. The enemy wore a uniform. Ships flew flags identifying who they were. Even in civil or revolutionary wars, you could identify the enemy. Now the enemy flies a plane into a building or releases nerve gas in the subways. The people or organizations we choose see civilian populations as their primary targets instead of collateral damage, so which side of that equation do you think the civilian population would rather be on? You're going to have blood on your hands if you don't act, so the only choice left is whether its theirs or yours. When the Squad goes out, the end result is *less* blood spilled, not more.

LUDLUM: So again, you're justifying Mrs. Waller and the Squad's actions by "adapting" the limits to meet your own utilitarian moral principles. Just war principles aren't real limits for you or her because you'll change them as often as modern military circumstances change. Does that fact that your moral principles don't actually impose *real* limits keep you up at night?

SMITH: I sleep well enough at night because I know you won't come up with a better answer than the one I have now. I suspect Mrs. Waller sleeps just fine as well. Unless you can do better, I suggest you go with what you got. With what works. The President is very pragmatic man and the Squad is a very pragmatic tool for dealing with real world, real politic situations. In my view.

LUDLUM: You weren't always of this view. You weren't always as compatible with Mrs. Waller, either, according to your file.

SMITH: I got to see her and the Squad in action and she and I have had many talks just like this one, You'll get used to her . . . and how she does business.

LUDLUM: We'll see. Moving on . . .

(*This ends the portion of the tape dealing with the Suicide Squad.*)

Phase Four

Beyond Good and Evil?

13

The Joker's Comedy
of Existence

DANIEL MOSELEY

> Dick Grayson . . . explained to me once that the Joker and I are for-
> ever linked in constant battle. That in some sick way, the Joker exists
> because of me. How I represent the order that is necessary to live in
> Gotham City and the Joker is the chaos that disrupts that order.
>
> —*Batman #614*, in *Hush*, Volume 2

Batman doesn't understand the Joker and Batman needs the help of
others to get insight into both the Joker's motivations and Batman's
own relationship to him. In *The Dark Knight* Alfred warns Bruce that,
like the mobsters who hired the Joker to kill Batman, Bruce may not
understand the man he is dealing with: "Some men aren't looking for
anything logical, like money. They can't be bought, bullied, or nego-
tiated with. Some men just want to watch the world burn."

In *The Killing Joke* a more experienced Batman echoes his frustrated attempts to understand the Joker: "I've been trying to figure
out what he intends to do. It's almost impossible. I don't know him,
Alfred. All these years and I don't know who he is any more than
he knows who I am. How can two people hate so much without
knowing each other?"

Batman expresses this idea again in his deadly conflict with the
Joker in *A Death in the Family* (where the Joker kills Jason Todd,
the second Robin): "We've been linked together so long, neither of
us truly understand the bond."

One challenge facing any discussion of the Joker involves determining which representations of the Joker are relevant. "The Clown
Prince of Crime" and the Dark Knight Detective have been at war
with each other since the Joker's first appearance in *Batman #1*

(1940) and their fighting has no end in sight. Batman and the Joker have been depicted in myriad, and not always consistent, ways in comic books, graphic novels, television shows and movies since their first encounter. Adam West and Christian Bale present radically different versions of the Dark Knight, and Cesar Romero's portrayal of the Joker does not fit with any depiction of the Joker that has appeared in film or print since 1985.

We'll focus on depictions of the Joker in *Batman #1* (which was recently reprinted in *The Joker: The Greatest Stories Ever Told*), the movie *The Dark Knight*, and the graphic novels, *A Death in the Family*, *The Killing Joke*, and *Batman: The Dark Knight Returns*. If you consider these stories as an integrated narrative, they present a compelling and coherent picture of the Joker. The picture that emerges from this narrative presents us with a perspective that you probably could not safely encounter face to face in the real world. The Joker was right when he said in his first appearance that if you're playing with the Joker, you "had best be prepared to be dealt from the bottom of the deck."

Batman's Struggle to Understand the Joker

Batman's crusade against crime is motivated by a vow: "I made a promise on the grave of my parents that I would rid this city of the evil that took their lives." In the epigraph to this chapter, Batman reflects on how he represents the order that is necessary to live in Gotham and the Joker represents the chaos that disrupts that order. So the Joker represents the evil that the Caped Crusader has sworn to eliminate from Gotham City and the Joker also represents the chaos that disrupts the order that is required to live in Gotham.

Political stability, public safety, and moral order are some of the key ingredients to having at least a minimally decent life in any city. The moral order that is required for such a life involves, among other things, at least protecting the basic rights of the citizens of that city and it also involves protecting public welfare. Batman represents the kind of order that is necessary to live in Gotham: an order that is established and maintained by *morality* and *reason*. The Dark Knight Detective is often praised by Alfred and others for his amazing reasoning skills and Batman is traditionally represented as embracing a reasonable and morality driven perspective (for an alternative depiction of Batman check out *Batman: The Dark Knight Returns*).

The Joker personifies the evil that took the lives of Batman's parents (Tim Burton's 1989 version of the movie *Batman* illustrated this point by making the Joker the man who murdered Bruce Wayne's parents—"Have you ever danced with the devil in the pale moon light?"). The Joker also embodies the chaos that disrupts the moral and political order that is necessary to live in Gotham. In *The Dark Knight* the Joker's wave of terror pressures Batman towards his decision to violate the privacy of the citizens of Gotham by tapping their cell phones in order to track down the Joker. So, the Joker's terrorism pressured Batman to violate the privacy rights of the citizens of Gotham in order to promote public welfare and political stability. The Joker has a talent for creating conflict in Batman's life and in the lives of everyone else in Gotham. The Joker represents evil and irrationality.

Not only does the Joker represent evil, the Joker is an evil person! To give a sense of what I mean by saying that the Joker is *evil* it helps to consider some examples. Examples of evil actions and evil people abound in history books, literature, movies, the daily news and graphic novels. Stories of serial killers, rapists and genocidal fanatics provide relatively uncontroversial examples of evil.

The Joker's life is loaded with examples of it. He has driven Harley Quinn and Harvey Dent insane. He shot Barbara Gordon in the spine, took pictures of her injured, naked body and then used those pictures in a terrifying circus show that was intended to drive Jim Gordon insane—Jim Gordon kept his sanity but Barbara's injury ended her career as Batgirl. The Joker also murdered Lieutenant Sarah Essen (Jim Gordon's wife) and he's murdered untold thousands of other people. The Joker has played the role of domestic terrorist: during his rein of terror in *The Dark Knight* he blew up a hospital, shut down Gotham City and placed two ferries in a twisted prisoner's dilemma. The Joker has also tried out international terrorism. In *A Death in the Family*, the Joker replaces emergency food supplies going to starving people in Ethiopia with his laughing venom: "Just imagine the surprise when one of your bleeding heart social workers opens any of these cartons. Each box contains enough gas to cover a four acre stretch. Just consider it my little contribution to the war against hunger." Kidnapping, torture, terrorism, rampage murders . . . the Joker has done it all.

Since it's so obvious that the Joker is evil, why does Batman have so much trouble understanding the Joker? It seems that Batman could easily explain the Joker's motives and character by

pointing out that he is an evil villain or that he is insane. One reason that Batman is probably not satisfied with these explanations is
because it's just too easy to explain the Joker's character and
motives by saying that he's evil or insane. There are different ways
of being evil and there are different ways of being insane. A more
specific characterization of the Joker's motives and evaluative outlook would help us (and Batman!) to understand the Joker. What's
the nature of the Joker's insanity? How is his insanity related to the
types of evil and chaos that he represents?

Desiring the Bad

You might think that the Joker is not evil, because, from his perspective, he thinks that his own actions are good. This suggests that
the Joker does not simply choose to do things because those things
are evil; rather the Joker has his own values and reasons for doing
things. It's true that the Joker has his own system of values and
those values rarely abide by the standards of conventional morality. However, a person does not have to think that their own
actions are evil in order for those actions to be evil. Some people
are *morally ignorant*: when they act, they think that their actions
are good and morally permissible when in fact those actions are
immoral. For instance, Harvey Dent may think that he has a moral
obligation to shoot an innocent child if his coin lands bad-side up,
but he is mistaken about what his moral obligations are—there is
no moral justification for murdering a child over a coin toss.

The Joker does not seem to be morally ignorant because he
knows that many of his monstrous deeds, such as mass murder, are
evil. He seems to devise many of his diabolical schemes *because*
they are evil. He brings a more difficult kind of case into view. The
Joker presents a character that one might call a *moral monster*:
moral monsters know that what they are doing is wrong, but they
go ahead and do it anyway. Moral monsters *knowingly* choose to
do things that are evil. Moreover, moral monsters are different than
sociopaths. Sociopaths have no conception of right and wrong;
they have no conscience. By contrast, moral monsters have a *corrupt* conscience.

The Joker seems to be a moral monster because he seems to do
many things, for instance: kill an audience of hundreds of people
with his Joker venom, because doing so is an evil thing to do. The
Joker seems to be a moral monster and there is a puzzle about

moral monsters that makes them particularly difficult to understand. This puzzle pertains to the challenging philosophical topic of *desiring the bad*. The puzzle asks, "Do moral monsters want to do what is evil because they think that their actions are bad or do moral monsters want to do what is evil because they think that their actions are good?" In other words, do evil people want to do what is evil *under the guise of the bad* or do they want to do what is evil *under the guise of the good?*

The most plausible answer that I see to this question draws from the arguments of the philosophers G.E.M. Anscombe and T.M. Scanlon. Their arguments suggest that desiring something consists in having a tendency to regard that thing as good. So, if I want to read *The Killing Joke* tonight, then I tend to regard reading *The Killing Joke* tonight in a positive light. So, evil people want to do evil things *under the guise of the good*. Evil people find some positive value (that is, they do see some good) in their actions. For instance, the Joker tends to attribute positive value to the pleasure that he gets from watching his victims' faces freeze into a demented smile from his Joker venom.

However, the goodness (or positive value) that evil people see in their action is not a form of *moral goodness*. As Satan of Milton's *Paradise Lost* cried, "Evil be Thou my Good!" Some moral monsters choose to do what is evil because they embrace a type of aesthetic perspective that attempts to bring non-moral and higher forms of goodness into the world via acts of cruelty or sadism. Moral monsters who have this type of aesthetic outlook often see the world as completely meaningless and devoid of value, or perhaps they see the world as full of mediocre forms of value. If the Joker is a moral monster, then perhaps he too has an inverted scheme of values and a rationale for having them!

The Joker and the Comedy of Existence

If the Joker has a rationale for his twisted values, then that means his actions will exhibit a certain kind of consistency because his actions will be motivated by those values. So what pattern of consistency is exhibited by the Joker's actions? One possibility is a love for showmanship. From the Joker's first encounter with Batman all the way back in *Batman #1* to his campaign of terror in *The Dark Knight*, the Joker uses the media to announce to Gotham City that he is going to perform some horrible crime. Many versions of his origin story describe the Joker using the media to publicize his shocking crimes. True to his persona as a *clown*, the Joker's acts of violence are performed out of a spirit of showmanship—a spirit of showmanship that unfortunately has also been displayed in actual cases of "rampage killers" (such as the Zodiac killer).

Although the Joker likes to draw a huge audience to witness his "artistic" endeavors, he also hates "the crowd" and their mediocrity—that is probably why he also usually tries to kill off his audience. He seems to strive towards a conception of his own personal excellence and he consistently attempts to overcome mediocrity, which is part of what his fans love about him. The Joker *embraces* the fact that ordinary people think that he's a freak, and he in turn rejects their conventional morality and conventional conceptions of justice.

The Joker aspires to what the philosopher Friedrich Nietzsche calls "higher values" and he calls for a "revaluation of values." The Joker, in his own way, asks us to think of *evil* as good and think of *justice* and *morality* as bad. The Joker also affirms the value of creativity and the value of his own authenticity. He is committed to his own conception of beauty and artistic values and he thinks that those values outweigh any considerations of morality and justice.

The Killing Joke provides us with an eloquent statement of the Joker's aspirations for "higher values." During an attempt to drive Jim Gordon insane, the Joker says:

> Ladies and Gentleman! You've read the newspapers! Now, shudder as you observe, before your very eyes, that most rare and tragic of nature's mistakes! I give you . . . the average man! Physically unremarkable, it has instead a deformed set of values. Notice the hideously bloated sense of humanity's importance. The club-footed social conscience and the withered optimism. It's certainly not for the squeamish is it? Most repulsive of all, are its frail and useless notions of order and sanity if too much weight is placed upon them . . . they snap. How does it live, I hear you ask? How does this poor, pathetic specimen survive in today's harsh and irrational world? The sad answer is "not very well." Faced with the inescapable fact that human existence is mad, random, and pointless, one in eight of them crack up and go stark slavering buggo! Who can blame them? In a world as psychotic as this . . . any other response would be crazy!

Here we get a glimpse into why the Joker strives for "higher values" and a "revaluation of values"—he thinks that human existence is irrational and insane! The Joker is trying to drive Jim Gordon insane in order to prove his point that human existence is irrational and insane.

Many philosophers have explored the idea that human reasoning is incapable of grasping reality and that our attempts to understand the world with reason are *absurd*. Albert Camus is frequently associated with the early twentieth century existentialists, but he considered himself an "absurdist." In his famous study of the Absurd called *The Myth of Sisyphus*, Camus writes, "The world in itself is not reasonable, that is all that can be said. But what is absurd is the confrontation of this irrational and the wild longing for clarity whose call echoes in the human heart." The Joker affirms this idea and he imbues his life with meaning by embracing irrationality and trying to foil Batman's attempts to have Gotham make sense.

Camus says, "There have always been men to defend the rights of the irrational," and the Joker is definitely one of those men. (Another might be the Comedian from *The Watchmen*.) Once again, in *The Killing Joke* (my favorite Joker story!), the Joker unleashes a direct and focused attack on reason:

> Memory's so treacherous. One moment you're lost in a carnival of delights with poignant childhood aromas, the flashing neon of puberty, all that sentimental candy-floss . . . the next, it leads you somewhere you don't want to go . . . somewhere dark and cold, filled with the damp, ambiguous shapes of things you'd hoped were forgotten. Memories can be vile, repulsive little brutes, like children, I suppose. Ha Ha. But can we live without them? Memories are what our reason is based upon. If we can't face them, then we deny reason itself! Although, why not? We aren't contractually tied down to rationality. There is no sanity clause! So when you find yourself locked onto an unpleasant train of thought, heading for the places in your past where the screaming is unbearable, remember there's always madness. Madness is the emergency exit... you can just step outside, and close the door on all those dreadful things that happened. You can lock them away . . . forever.

There are two important philosophical points here. First, the Joker is asking us to abandon our memories and voluntarily choose insanity. The Joker claims that memory cannot be relied upon, because it is unreliable and it can lead us to horrible thoughts that should not be remembered. (This point makes you wonder what the Joker has been through. Similarly, in *The Dark Knight* the Joker tells inconsistent stories about where he got his scars. Wherever and however he got them, it must have been horrible.) Perhaps the Joker's own memory is unreliable, but that is very weak evidence for thinking that either everyone else or most other people have unreliable memory. If you have somewhat reliable memory, then the Joker's point does not apply to you. Also, most of us have memories of our past that make us who we are, in an important sense, and those memories give our lives meaning. Memory is required to sustain our friendships and other bonds of loyalty. How could the Joker maintain his relationship with Batman if he *completely* forgot his past?

Second, the Joker's argument is interesting but it is self-defeating. If the Joker is trying to convince us that reality is irrational and that we cannot rely on the power of reason, why has he given us an *argument* for that claim? By providing arguments for his claim that reality is irrational and crazy, he is using *reasoning* to make his point. One general problem facing any philosophical defense of irrationalism is that philosophical defenses require *arguments* and good arguments require good reasoning. If you believe that reality is irrational, then it is hard to see how that belief could be justified and if the belief is unjustified (and irrational) then you have no reason to believe it. Like many other aspects of the Joker's personality, this defense of absurdism is at odds with itself.

The Joker's Obsession with Batman

The Joker's irrationality also manifests itself in his obsession with Batman. This obsession fragments the Joker's will. When Batman foils one of the Joker's heists in *Batman #1*, the Joker yells, "I'm going to kill you!" and in *The Dark Knight* the Joker is hired by Gotham City's top mobsters to kill the Batman. Usually the Joker tries to kill Batman when the opportunity arises. However, the Joker also seems to love Batman in a sick kind of way—the Joker's struggle with Batman imbues his life with value and meaning. After Batman abruptly ends a conversation with the Joker in *A Death in the Family*, the Joker says, "Gone! I hate it when he does that. But he does make life worth living." The Joker also alludes to the deep significance he finds in his struggle with Batman in *The Dark Knight*.

> I don't wanna kill you! What would I do *without* you? Go back to ripping off mob dealers? No. No. You *complete me*. . . .

> You won't kill me because of some misplaced sense of self-right-
> eousness, and I won't kill you because . . . you're just too much fun.
> I've got the feeling that you and I are destined to do this forever.

So, here we see that the Joker has an irrational set of desires. He
wants to kill Batman and he wants to keep fighting with him forever. The Joker's relationship with Batman is a type of volitional
inconsistency—he wants to kill Batman and he wants to continue
fighting Batman forever. But doesn't everyone have inconsistent
desires? If so, are we all irrational and insane? Everyone probably
has some inconsistent desires. I want to eat the cupcakes in my
kitchen and I also do not want to eat them (I'm on a diet).
However, this type of volitional inconsistency is not clearly irrational or insane. (Determining the nature of irrationality and insanity are challenging philosophical issues. Are certain desires
inherently irrational? Or, is irrationality primarily a matter of the
relations between desires? Which forms of irrationality are also
forms of insanity?) One reason that the Joker's volitional inconsistency seems irrational and insane is that it involves a tension
between his *deep* desires, which are desires that are involved in his
understanding of who he is and what matters most to him. The
Joker's obsession with Batman is a particularly problematic form of
irrationality, because his obsession involves conflicting desires
about the most important thing in his life—his relationship with
Batman.

In the Dark

Why does Batman remain in the dark when it comes to understanding the Joker? These reflections suggest that Batman's overly
rational and moral perspective prevents him from seeing the essential *irrationality* of the Joker's point of view. The Joker's disdain for
mediocrity, his rejection of naive convention and his desire to see
the world as it really is are the wellspring of his villainy but they
are also the qualities of great philosophers. On the other side of the
coin, does the Joker understand Batman? The Joker often tries to
show Batman the *absurdity* of the Caped Crusader's own costumed
and illegal vigilante war against crime. Occasionally the Joker gets
through to Batman: consider the laugh that Batman and the Joker
have together in the last two pages of *The Killing Joke*. However,
Batman usually remains in the dark about their relationship.

How will things end with Batman and the Joker? *Batman: The Dark Knight Returns* describes one, particularly grim, possible future for the Dark Knight and the Clown Prince of Crime. There Batman does finally end his relationship with the Joker by non-fatally breaking his neck. In his final act of will the Joker finishes the job and kills himself in order to make sure that Batman is blamed for his death. Once the Joker is dead, Batman's despotic streak emerges as he creates a vigilante league whose purpose is to keep order in Gotham City. Without the Joker in the picture, Batman's desire for order seems to devolve into a desire for tyranny. Perhaps the Joker serves as a kind of mirror image for Batman: the Joker keeps Batman's uncompromising rationality in check and Batman checks the Joker's irrationalism. These issues may be difficult to resolve. However, as Batman says at the end of *A Death in the Family*, "That's the way things always end with the Joker and me. Unresolved."[1]

---

[1] I would like to thank Ben Dyer for helpful feedback on earlier versions of this chapter and thank Joseph Milton and Sam Duncan for engaging conversations about the topics discussed here.

14
Mutation and Moral Community

NOAH LEVIN

In the coolest scene in the *X-Men* movie series, Magneto extracts liquid metal from the blood of his prison guard and escapes in a way that would probably amaze even the dead guard if it wasn't happening to him. Wolverine can heal instantaneously, Mystique can shape shift, and Professor X can read thoughts. Because of these amazing powers, Magneto claims that mutants are morally superior to non-mutants. In the "I, Magneto" back story published in *Classic X-Men* #19 (1988), Magneto himself best describes his views:

> Little man, have you no notion who you're dealing with? I am *Homo superior*—the next generation of humanity, heir apparent to this paltry planet. As Cro-Magnon supplanted Neanderthal . . . so shall we, you . . . You are like children—intellect and power without the maturity to use either responsibly, unfit to rule lives or world. Better to be *ruled* instead . . . by one who shall make sure you know—and keep—your place . . . It is *I* who shall lead my people to the glory they deserve. I, *Übermensch*. I, *mutant*! I–MAGNETO!

Are mutants actually superior to non-mutants or are they just a little different, and what exactly *does* it mean to be superior? Are you superior if your mutant power is just making someone smell bad or stand on their head? Would having such a power make someone *morally* superior? All that matters to Magneto is that one belongs to the mutant species, but he might think differently given a little philosophical reflection on biology and morality.

Mutant Biology

No one would doubt that Magneto has some truly amazing powers and that he is physically superior to many people, but the basis of his elitism is his mutant nature. Even the amazing Rust, who has the unremarkable power to make metal rust, would be superior simply because he is a mutant. But what makes a mutant a mutant? A mutant is simply anyone that has an activated X-gene (also known as the X-factor). Normally, physiological changes in the body, such as puberty, cause the X-gene to be expressed. Although everyone actually has the X-gene (it was implanted in all humans by cosmic beings called the Celestials during human pre-history), it is dormant in most people. After years of speculation and problematic scientific explanations of how mutants actually get their powers, *Astonishing X-Men #25* finally explained, once and for all, how the X-gene works . . . sort of.

Although the explanation has some serious defects, it can form the basis of a biologically plausible explanation. While testing a person's DNA, Beast explains how mutants like the X-Men work.

> We all have two sets of chromosomes, and they're full of genes. The term for this is diploid. The X-gene always sits on Chromosome 23, and uses an exotic protein to send chemical signals to the other genes, which mutates them. Hence, us.

Let's call this exotic protein the "X-protein". Although this is a very brief explanation, and there are still a few gaps that need to be filled in before this can become a fully reasonable and working explanation of mutation, it's now much clearer how mutants actually work.

The *Astonishing X-Men* series comes after *House of M* and *Decimation* in which Scarlet Witch (Wanda Maximoff) almost eliminated all expressions of the X-gene on M-day. Most mutants lost their powers and devolved into normal human beings once the X-gene was deactivated in their bodies. Some mutants maintained their altered appearance but lost their powers. It's unclear whether the X-gene was actually eliminated or merely made inactive, but if Beast's explanation is to be believed, then mutants that lost their powers have not lost their X-genes. However, there's a problem here—if the X-gene mutates genes as Beast described, then mutants should not have lost their powers when the X-gene was removed or made inactive. Understanding why this is so requires that we first delve into a little bit of genetic theory.

Genes contain the basic biological information for our bodies. They are the blueprints for our body and our bodies are built in accord with their instructions. The information in our genes that dictates our biological characteristics is called our genotype, but there is more that goes into who we are than just our genotype because environmental factors influence the expression of our genes. For example, the nutrition we receive as we develop can alter the physical traits we exhibit such as height or weight. The set of actual traits that we do exhibit is called our phenotype. While my genotype indicates I should have a left arm, if I lost an arm in an accident, my phenotype would include having just one arm.

Perhaps an easy way of thinking about the distinction is that a genotype is like the blueprints for a building, and the phenotype is an actually existing building built from those blueprints. The building may constantly change, but the basic design remains the same. There could also be multiple buildings that gradually become unique over time even though they were based on the same blueprints. This is exactly the way identical twins become distinguishable both physically and psychologically as they grow older. They have the same genotype, but different phenotypes.

To return to the topic at hand, Beast describes the X-protein as mutating other genes. When a cell replicates, it duplicates all of its genes and creates exact copies in its daughter cells. So if a mutation occurs in one cell, then its daughter cells will carry the same mutation. Cancer cells are a perfect example of how this can work—a cell becomes cancerous through a mutation, and then multiplies constantly with its mutations. Once a gene is mutated by the X-protein, then it should remain so even once the X-gene and X-protein have disappeared. If the X-protein actually directly modifies the DNA of a gene, then that change is permanent, regardless of whether or not the X-gene or X-protein remains in the body.

There is a possible explanation for how the X-gene could work in the fashion Beast describes *and* be consistent with the events of M-day. In addition to the X-gene being neutralized in some fashion, the DNA of every mutant must have been changed back to the pre-mutation genome while leaving intact the outward physical changes that some mutants maintained. However, we have no reason to think the changes on M-day were this involved and complex, so I will dismiss this as unlikely. If mutants lost their powers when the X-protein left their system, then the X-gene and X-protein must work in some other way. So how can the X-protein change genes and be required for mutations to remain?

There is one simple and plausible explanation: the X-protein modifies the *expression* of susceptible genes. Think of it as a type of "genetic enhancer." Magneto's powers could be explained by the idea that we all have genes that allow us to subtly sense magnetic fields (similar to abilities found in sharks) that when magnified by the X-protein endows one with the ability to expertly sense and modify magnetic fields. Similar explanations could extend to all mutants. While their genotypes would remain the same, their phenotypes would be altered and enhanced through the X-protein modifying genetic expression.

One interesting implication of this method of mutation is that if the X-protein is identical across individuals (as most proteins are), then the protein could be isolated, replicated, and implanted into non-mutants to make them mutate. To actually be a mutant, you wouldn't need an activated X-gene; you would only require a fresh supply of any mutant's X-proteins. Of course, if X-proteins are unique for each individual mutant, then, for you to be a mutant, you would require your own unique activated X-gene. But this is highly unlikely because most proteins are identical across individuals (and those that do differ are only very slightly different). The existence and function of the X-protein has important implications for mutant elitism—if everyone can become a mutant with the proper protein, then why are mutants so special? Before we get to that, let's stop for a moment and take stock of what our survey of mutant biology teaches us.

To be a genetic mutant, a person must have a modified genetic code, but the genes do not actually undergo modification when the X-gene becomes activated. They are thus not mutants in the normal sense that we might think of them. That is, despite the fact that not everyone expresses it, because mutants *and normal humans* possess the X-gene, Marvel's mutants do not really count as having genetic mutations. The other genes in their human DNA that result in "mutations" also are not mutated genes because only the expressions of those genes are different. In short, humans and mutants have the same genotype, but different phenotypes. Thus, we might think of Marvel's mutants as "phenotypic mutants" rather than genotypic mutants. They can still be considered mutants because their genes are expressed in a mutated fashion by of the X-protein even while the genes themselves remain constant.

Homo sapiens superior?

Now we have a definition of what makes a mutant a mutant—an activated X-gene, which produces the X-protein, which then enhances susceptible genes. So what does this mean for mutant kind? Are they a different species or still just normal humans with some cool abilities?

Mutants are known as *Homo sapiens superior* in the X-men universe, which means they are part of the *Homo sapiens* species but are the subspecies *superior*. (Humans are *Homo sapiens sapiens*.) This biological classification of mutants means that they would not be a unique species. Instead, they would be a distinct group of individuals derived from the primary (nominate) species. Can this classification be correct?

If the X-gene is present in all *Homo sapiens*, then there is *no* genetic variation that mutants share that would make them a distinct subspecies. It is clear that mutants are definitely part of the human species, especially since they can reproduce with non-mutants and produce fertile offspring, but there is nothing that indicates they should be considered a subspecies. It is simply wrong to think of them as a unique subspecies because mutants are genetically identical before and after expressing the X-gene.

If mutants are not a unique subspecies, then what are they? They're simply humans that have been enhanced in some way. Mutant abilities range drastically in both effects (Mystique's shapechanging, Blob's immobility, or Sabretooth's healing) and power (Magneto's magnetic abilities versus Polaris's). Mutants like the Morlocks suffer from only minor physical deformities and have *no* major powers. It's even possible some mutants die when under the effects of the X-protein. Though all mutants share the fact their X-gene has been activated, they share little or nothing else in common that would identify them as a separate species.

Magneto is the most outspoken supporter of the separation of mutants and non-mutants. He fluctuates between being an elitist and merely a separatist (after all, he does not want anyone to experience the hatred he experienced during the Holocaust), but he is always advocating for mutant-kind over and above non-mutants. Others, such as the High Evolutionary and Apocalypse, also advocate for some form of mutant superiority at various times. But what exactly is the basis for this elitism and are they justified in holding such views?

The basis for elitism is simple: mutants are better than normal, non-mutated humans because they either have superior abilities or are the next step in human evolution, and usually it is both. These motivations are present in varying degrees at different times, and both are based on the notion that mutants exhibit qualities that make them more important. We're now in a position to measure this elitism based on the biological facts of mutation. We have observed that mutants are genetically no different from humans, so genetic mutation cannot be a justifiable basis for their elitism. Can phenotypic mutation justify elitism instead? Again, the answer should be "no" because there is no *consistent* phenotypic variation across individuals as evidenced by the fact that mutants vary greatly in their abilities.

Thus, there is no categorical difference that separates mutants from non-mutants. All that mutants have is an activated X-gene, and there is no reason to think that mutants are superior merely for that reason. Nonetheless, if mutants are not categorically superior to humans, can some mutants be superior merely in virtue of their enhanced abilities? In one sense, it is easy to see that Colossus has superior strength relative to a normal human, but Magneto is making a claim about *moral* superiority. Does the fact that some mutants have powers mean that they are morally superior?

The Nature of Moral Communities

No one would doubt that every mutant is in some way superior to everyone else, but this is true for normal human beings as well. Most people have something at which they excel and can do better than many others, so this is probably not the sense in which Magneto feels mutants are superior to non-mutants. Magneto sees mutants as categorically superior because they are like gods (or at least angels) to non-mutants. This is the basis of his belief in mutants' moral superiority, and he thinks that mutants are better than humans in the same way that humans consider themselves better than other animals. Biologically speaking, mutants are not better than (nor really any different from) non-mutants simply because of their X-proteins, but can they be of a different *moral* kind than non-mutants?

In order to understand the moral place of mutants, we must examine something called a "moral community" and the characteristics that place one in a moral community. A moral community is a group of individuals who have certain moral obligations to or expectations from other members. For example, the philosopher Immanual Kant believed that the ability to have rational thought was necessary to act morally. Thus, any being that thinks rationally is capable of morality and is part of the "moral community" in every possible way. Other philosophers offer different criteria to distinguish the moral community's members, and who is included and how it works can vary. But there are some general features that most accounts share in common.

Members of a moral community can be generally classed into two groups—moral patients and moral agents. A moral patient is a member of the community that can be acted upon in a morally significant manner. A moral agent is a member that can be, and is expected to, act in a morally correct fashion. Most moral agents are also moral patients, but not all moral patients are moral agents. For example, many people would consider sentient animals to be moral patients even though they are not also moral agents. Certain characteristics place someone or something in a moral community as either a patient or an agent, and it is possible to think that some members have partial membership or that the members can be ranked in importance. However it is described, there are morally significant differences among the various members of the moral community: we would probably extend some amount of membership to a rabid wolf and a playful puppy, but we treat them both differently from each other, and certainly different from another human being.

On most views, what makes someone a full member of the moral community, a *person* in the philosopher's sense, is that one is capable of a certain level of intelligence and rationality coupled with some amount of free will. What this means is that from Namor the Atlantean *Homo mermanus* to Superman the Kryptonian, anyone capable of rational agency deserves the fullest moral consideration and is expected to return that same consideration to others. This is because any being that shares our own kind of psychological complexity can be held morally responsible for their actions in ways that less sophisticated creatures cannot. Thus, persons have certain obligations to other full members of the moral community that might not extend to creatures that are only partially in that community. For example, we might have an obligation to risk harm to ourselves to save another person, but we might not have that obligation towards a cow.

With this conception of moral community in hand, we can now consider what it means for mutants to be members of our moral community of persons. For any moral community, there will be a set of characteristics that determine an individual's membership in that community. If you have them, you're a member, and if you don't, then you're not—no exceptions. Mutants fulfill the requirements for full membership in the moral community of persons as we've described them because they exhibit all of the relevant psychological characteristics. Thus, mutants should be treated in the same moral fashion as any other persons as far our discussion of moral community is concerned. For that reason, the Mutant Registration Act would be highly immoral.

Similarly, Magneto's actions would be immoral as well, even if he claims that he belongs to an entirely separate moral community based on his identity as a mutant. For Magneto to be correct, he would have to specify morally relevant characteristics that pick out a unique moral community comprised exclusively of mutants. However, because there is no categorical way in which mutants are different from non-mutants (except for the activated X-gene, which we've already seen cannot justifiably ground elitism), it would seem that what makes one mutant a part of another mutant's moral community will be just the same psychological characteristics that make a mutant or a non-mutant a full member of the moral community of persons. In that case, there's no reason to think that mutants in the X-men universe should be members of a different and superior moral community.

Distinctions Without a Difference

The mutants in the X-men universe are clearly different from non-mutants. They frequently have powers that we non-mutants can only get in video games, our imagination, dreams, or, if we're lucky, through some cool technology (like Iron Man). Yet mutants and humans share more similarity than difference. They all need to eat, obey the laws, pay taxes, worry about what to wear (some mutants should pay more attention to this one), get depressed, feel happy, feel sad, feel for other people, and so on.

Mutants can be so different from humans that they might truly seem to be members of a different species, but most mutants simply do not have such radical variation in power or appearance. Although Magneto exhibits a very powerful ability, it is one that has been taken away (he lost it after M-day) and restored (in one case by the High Evolutionary) without changing his essential moral outlook. This suggests that when it comes down to it, Magneto is no different in any morally significant way from the humans to whom he is so condescending. This should come as no surprise to us since, after all, he is, was, and remains just another flawed human being.

15
Two Fates for Two-Face

DENNIS O'NEIL

We have no need to hurry, but let's do it anyway—orient ourselves with the golden compass and rush into our journey. Look at the places we pass: Utopia, Never Never Land, Wonderland, Narnia, Middle Earth, Lilliput, and—we're getting close to our destination— Cimmeria and Hogwarts and . . . we take a sharp left, zoom past Metropolis and find ourselves in Gotham City. Do we have to worry about what year it is? No. Time, as it's reckoned in our native region, is infinitely malleable and almost nonexistent here. So all we have to do is focus on a character.

Harvey Dent: he's our man!

Or rather, our boy. We find Harvey in church, a Presbyterian church, to be exact, at age . . . oh, let's say eleven. He's kneeling, as always, in the front row, hands folded, eyes cast upward. None of this staring-at-the-floor nonsense, not for Harvey. He's look the Almighty straight in the eye, thank you very much, and though all he's actually seeing is a plaster ceiling with a jagged crack running from one wall to another, he is certain the Almighty is smiling down on him.

Young Master Dent, as it happens, is *filled* with certainty. He knows that he will get straight A's on his next report card and that the teachers will continue to love him and that Dad will tousle his hair and Mom will call him her fine, big, hero and Harvey knows— he doesn't merely think, he *knows*—that he is among those the Lord has decreed already saved, his place in heaven already warmed up and waiting for him. Of course, he also knows that he must serve the Lord because that's why the Lord placed him on the Earth and he's pretty sure he has a way to do it, a way to please both the Lord and his parents—a way that gives him a feeling so righteous that is must be the *correct* way. He will become a lawyer, Harvey will, just like his idol, John Calvin, whose theology is what makes the world a sane place for Harvey. He will serve the Lord by punishing sinners! What could be better? More noble?

Because we are not constrained by chronology, and only minimally by logic, we don't have to witness every second of Harvey's adolescence: every moment of triumph—another round of straight A's,—or of humiliation—why *wouldn't* she go to the prom with him?—or of banality—another trip to the bathroom. Instead, we are in strobe mode and our view of Harvey's world can is seen in flashes, as though lit by lightning, or like the panels in a comic strip.

Let's very briefly look at him standing on the school steps minutes after his eighth grade graduation, clutching a diploma—the first of many—and surrounded by smiling family. His uncle Gerald beams down at Harvey from over a large belly and hands him a fifty-cent piece with two heads. *So you'll always be lucky*, Gerald says, and laughs his rumbling laugh. Harvey knows there's no such thing as luck, not really. What people call luck is merely the Lord's approval. But the coin is interesting and Harvey sees nothing wrong with keeping it.

His life continues, one triumph after another. Class valedictorian! College swim team! Law school . . .

No, before we follow Harvey into postgraduate life, let's pause and meet him in the library, where he is studying for an exam in the one elective course he's taking this semester. History of Philosophy, it's called, and it is not what Harvey expected. He thought he would learn more about such philosophical giants as Jonathan Edwards, John Calvin's explicator, whose magnificent sermon *Sinners in the Hands of an Angry God* was the most moving and exciting work Harvey had ever read. Instead, the course presents lies as though they were truths, or at least as though they *might* be truths. Harvey loathes it. "What nonsense," he mutters, unaware that he's spoken aloud, or that the freckle-faced girl across the table is staring at him. This philosophy stuff is baloney, which Harvey should have known from reading the syllabus. What had he been thinking? Why learn *false* ideas when he already knew the truth? He's particularly insulted by the section on the Existentialists. No, not insulted . . . *offended!* This Frenchman, this atheist Sartre and his assertion that man is "condemned to freedom." Drivel! Why not quote Lewis Carroll and say that man is a slivey tove who gyres

and gimbols in the wabe. . . . That would make as much sense—
more sense.

Harvey slams the textbook closed, startling the freckle-faced
girl, and marches to the registrar's office, where he withdraws from
the course. At home, he flings the textbook into the back of a closet
where it rests amid old tennis shoes and a broken umbrella.

He gets an "incomplete" for the course, the only blemish on an
otherwise perfect academic record.

But not the only bump in his particular academic road. We're
now seeing Harvey, whose face is paler than usual, standing beside
his chair in a lecture hall, speaking loudly to a thin man with thick
glasses and wisps of white hair combed over a spotty scalp. The
man is a history professor, and his face, in contrast to Harvey's,
appears unnaturally ruddy as he shouts back at Harvey. They're
arguing about the Inquisition, which the Professor terms an "abomination." Harvey says no, Torquemada and his Dominican cohorts
may have erred in certain particulars, but their cause and methods
were above reproach.

Later, leaving the building, Harvey turns to a thin, intense young
woman wearing a t-shirt and cargo pants and says, apropos of
nothing, that John Calvin co-operated with the Inquisition.

At that moment, in the faculty lounge, the professor is pouring
coffee from a thermos into a paper cup and telling a colleague that
he would love to flunk that little bastard Dent, but he can't. The little prick's exams were perfect and his written work, though drab
and boring, fulfilled the terms of the assignments exactly.

So the *incomplete* remains the only blemish on Harvey's tran-
script as he continues his triumphant procession through life. Law
school, and editorship of the law review and the Wayne Prize for
outstanding legal acumen and, inevitably, the trip to Washington,
up the wide marble steps into the Supreme Court and a clerkship
with one of the justices. He had gotten a lot of offers after graduation, from the whitest of white-shoe firms in Los Angeles, Chicago,
Seattle, New York, and, of course, Gotham City. But he wasn't
interested in either helping the rich get richer—if the Lord wanted
a person rich, Harvey thought, the Lord would see to the matter—
and even less interested in defending criminals. The very idea of
sitting at a defense table horrified him. Help sinners avoid their just
desserts? Utter depravity!

While he's still at the Supreme Court, he begins, again, to get
offers. Many, many offers of many different kinds. Firms from

dozens of United States cities, and from London, Paris, and Buenos Aires: *Come work for us and enjoy a six-figure salary that will become seven figures within five years and drive a company Porsche and golf at the country club . . .*

Law firms aren't the only ones making offers. Harvey is sometimes described as "movie-star handsome" and at other times as merely "extremely good looking." And he is a lawyer with a glittering future and his mentor is a Supreme Court Justice, and he's even polite, and so there is no more eligible bachelor in America than young Mr. Dent, Esq., and many women, all of them wealthy and most of them comely, constantly seek his company.

He really doesn't blame them. He *is* handsome, a fact he affirms often by examining himself in a full-length mirror next to his bed. Of course, what he's looking at is only his body, but he is convinced that his body is the mirror of his soul. If his *body* is this beautiful, surely his *soul* must rival the angels themselves.

After work, on his last day in the capital, Harvey's boss, the Justice, invites him into an inner sanctum for a little chat. The Justice tells Harvey that the nation needs men like him at the highest level and yes, he did mean Pennsylvania Avenue, men who understood true values, and with Harvey's education and, yes, his looks, there is no earthly reason why he couldn't shoot up like a rocket and call the White House home as early as Kennedy did, in his early forties, and do a heck of a lot more good than the rich snot from Massachusetts ever had.

They shake hands and Harvey gets a cab to Union Station, where a Metroliner will carry him home to Gotham.

He has accepted a position with the district attorney's office. Most of the Gotham legal community feels that this is a first, step for Harvey Dent, a necessary but very low and temporarily step, and that within a few years he'll either go into a big firm, private practice, or politics. Harvey isn't so sure. He imagined that he'd like prosecuting and once he actually does it, he discovers he loves it. He especially enjoys the expression on perps' faces when they realize that he *has* them, they are trapped, they are doomed, there is nothing they or their lawyers can do to save them. Jonathan Edwards put what Harvey feels best when he wrote of sinners that "hell is gaping for them, the flames gather and flash about them and would fain lay hold on them . . ." Yes, yes—the fate of those who have not the Lord's favor, the lost, the doomed. He thought of the evildoers languishing in prison, a foretaste of the hell that awaited them after death, and he remembered that Jonathan Edwards said that part of Heaven would be the awareness of the torment of those in Hell, and so surely he could preview his eternal reward by imagining the agonies of the penitentiary. Often, he would imagine what the words must have sounded like coming from Edwards's lips and then, facing a jury, imbue his own speech with the same fiery righteousness.

He is doing the Lord's work and the Lord is rewarding him with fame and honor upon honor.

The citizens of Gotham trust Harvey because he trusts himself. He speaks with the calmness and assurance of one who knows, absolutely, that he's right. And he is spectacularly good at his job. All those long hours in law school, the weekends spent hunched over fat texts while his classmates were debauching are serving him well. It seems as though he is incapable of error.

Then, he gets the opportunity of his young career. The local police have managed to stop stumbling over their own flat feet and put the cuffs on Salvatore Maroni, known, sometimes admiringly, as "Boss" Maroni. For a decade Maroni has been thumbing his nose, often literally, at law enforcers, both local and federal, and now, largely through the efforts of a new guy in the PD, one Lieutenant James Gordon, Maroni has slipped and is in jail awaiting trial on charges ranging from racketeering to murder. But the evidence against him is largely circumstantial and he has hired some of the best legal talent on the planet. The guys who hang around he courthouse think this one is anything but a slam-dunk. Harvey doesn't agree. He *knows* he will put Maroni in prison, if not on an execution gurney.

The trial begins. Harvey is addressing the jury, pacing back and forth between the jury box and the defendant's table, gesturing, speaking, holding the jury rapt and then, at the edge of his vision, he sees abrupt motion and there is a wetness on his face and then pain—enormous pain, and shouts, and cops tumbling over each other and Harvey is on his knees, and the pain is seeping down the front of his body.

He is in a hospital, head swathed in bandages, a plastic hose dripping morphine into his left arm. The drug makes him unable to think coherently, and only partially quells his agony.

Various people drift in and out of his room: white-jacketed medical personnel, clergymen, family friends, and cops. One of the city detectives, a taurine lump of a man named, appropriately, Bullock, has news. The GCPD has made a thorough investigation of what's become known as The Incident and, Bullock assures Dent, nothing could have been done because:

> *The cop who woulda patted Maroni down was late counta he forgot his gun and had to run back home to get it and then he was caught in traf-fic counta a steam pipe busting and when he finally gets to the court-house the trial's already late getting started and he just rushes Maroni in, ya can't blame him, and anyway the acid wasn't originally intended for you, Maroni was gonna use it on an ex-girlfriend only she was struck by lightning in the park and near as we can tell Maroni for-got he even had it in his pocket . . .*

All happenstance? All heedless luck?

But where were You? Harvey mumbles beneath his bandages, and waits for an answer. *Pray tell, where were You?*

Snipping off Harvey's bandages with a silvery scissors, the doctor tells him that he might be a bit . . . *dismayed* by what he's about to see. The last of the bandage is unwound, its inner sur-face soggy and discolored, and a nurse holds a round mirror up in front of Harvey's face. Harvey stares, says he's seen enough, asks if there are any small children around he might scare. The nurse and doctor are out of the room and halfway down the cor-ridor before they realize that Harvey Dent meant his last question as a joke. A nurse injects him with a drug that is supposed to induce sleep, but for some reason, it fails, and Harvey lies awake deep into the night, feeling hatred and a need to wreak vengeance upon the whole world—to rend, to destroy—and savoring the feelings.

His face swathed in bandages, he goes home. He happens to see himself in the hall mirror, winces, finds some old sheets in the cellar and cuts them into rectangles. Then he covers every mirror in the house.

Next, he finds a cardboard box on the kitchen table, left by a policeman. It contains what he was wearing and carrying when he was splashed with acid. Suit and tie and shirt, all damaged; a hole eaten through the left leg of his pants; wallet untouched; and last, the two-headed coin his uncle Gerald had given him years before. One side was completely unsullied, but the other . . . obviously, the acid had touched it and it was as defiled as Harvey himself. He stares at it, laying on the table, for a long time, feeling something ugly and alien swelling within him. He struggles to give it a name and finally, he can: *doubt*. He is doubting, for the first time in his life, but doubting *what?*

He awakes in the middle of the night knowing the answer, knowing the answer and because he knows it, feeling deep terror.

He is doubting everything.

And isn't a sin, this doubt? Isn't doubt the *first* sin? Didn't Adam and Eve doubt in the garden when the Lord told them that they were "free to eat from any tree in the garden, but you must not eat from the tree of knowledge of good and evil, for when you eat of it you will surely die." The sin—the crime!—was not in eating the apple, but in doubting the assurance of the Almighty regarding what would happen to them if they did.

Harvey did not *want* to doubt. Was this the Lord's way of sending him a message? Could Harvey have been wrong about his salvation? Was he one of the unsaved? Doomed to an eternity of torment?

But he was good! He had always obeyed the Commandments and the laws of man, too. Why should he be damned?

He had often found answers in books—answers and often solace. But he knows that his thick law books will tell him nothing he does not already know, nothing of use. He puts on a trench coat and pulls the collar up around his damaged face and walks three blocks to a small branch library. Inside, he wanders aimlessly among the stacks until he sees a science book. Harvey has never spent so much as an hour studying science because, he has always felt, Scripture contained all he needs to know about the workings of the world. He reads the book in one sitting and returns the next day to read another. That evening, when he returns to his room, he remembers the philosophy book he once threw into the back of his closet, with the tennis shoes and umbrella.

He reads it in an afternoon. The section on the existentialists holds him; these heathens claim that the universe has no intrinsic meaning and thus each man must make his own meaning, must *choose* what to believe. Harvey closes the book almost reverently, puts it aside, goes to the library and returns home with a stack of books on physics. This leads him to a biography of Albert Einstein and reading that leaves him horrified and fascinated. *God does not play dice with the universe,* the great man insisted, and yet for thirty years he tried and failed to prove this assertion. The evidence, some based on Einstein's own early work, indicated that on subatomic levels, much of reality *is* random.

It gets worse. Harvey reads, and feels revulsion curling within him; what these scientists say far exceeds blasphemy . . . *human observation determines reality*—human, *not divine... information depends on wave functions . . . new universes are constantly being created by quantum events . . .*

He closed the book and stared at the rug. That last thing—the constant creation of new universes—could that mean that some-where/somewhen, in some inaccessible reality, he was whole, unmaimed? Could there be many Harveys, each as real as the rest? Could there be trillions of Harvey Dent biographies, each different and each no less true than countless others? Is it possible that the Lord existed in some of these realities and not in others?

Doubt doubt doubt doubt . . . Harvey realizes that doubt has become part of him, has replaced his faith. He recalls something he read quickly and returns to the philosophy text. The chapter on Nietzsche . . . where is it? Ah—here!

> My formula for greatness in a human being is *amor fati*: that one wants nothing to be different, not forward, not backward, not in all eternity. Not merely to bear what is necessary, still less conceal it—but love it.

And suddenly, everything is clear. Harvey has a revelation, like Saul on the road to Damascus, but Harvey's enlightenment comes not from on high, from Heaven, if such exists, but from below, the depths of the Earth itself, this truth, which seizes Harvey's very being, has been obvious all the time—he first heard it in Sunday School. Man is dual, part angel and part animal, part good, part evil. Harvey's error was in denying this. Ah. But now . . . *Amor Fati!* Yes! And what better emblem than his own face, displaying both sides of his nature, angelic and demonic? Harvey is becoming excited. He runs through the house, uncovering the mirrors, hum-ming a tune, anxious to begin his new—his *real*—existence.

But how? What should he do? Good or bad? Life, he is now con-vinced, is utterly random. Then, a new and terrible question occurs to him: How can he make decisions? Suddenly, he remembers the words of the atheist Sartre, and understands: man *is* condemned to freedom! Harvey has always known what to do because he has always believed. But now? He sits at the kitchen table and his gaze falls upon the coin his uncle had given him, the two-faced half dol-lar, one side marred by the same acid that marred Harvey himself, and Harvey has his answer.

Good or bad? Should he succumb to the savage urges he feels within, or stifle them? Random chance, in the guise of the coin, will decide. He tosses it spinning into the air, catches it, looks: the damaged face. In another universe, maybe, a Harvey Dent was looking at an unmarred face, and would eventually find himself doing scut work in a windowless library in the rear of law office, and in another, maybe, a bird flew in the window and snatched the coin from the air, and in another. . . . But why speculate? It is *this* universe, *this* Harvey Dent, that concerns him, and in *this* universe . . .

Amor fati, baby.

Phase Five

Fiendish Puzzles

16

What Limits an All-Powerful Being?

CRAIG LINDAHL-URBEN and
CHARLES TALIAFERRO

They were taken against their will, heroes and villains alike, and sorted into two teams. Clustering together, they watched as an alien world was formed like some Frankenstein's monster from the living pieces of other worlds. All were kidnapped by an unfathomable entity from beyond the known universe, transported to this new world, and set in battle for the ultimate prize: all their desires fulfilled.

It's a scenario we've seen or imagined many times, but what makes this situation different is that it happened in the Marvel Universe decades ago. This was real old-school stuff from back when Reed Richards was in his forties, married to Sue, and not an eighteen year old wunderkind like he is now. It's an oldie but goodie, and it starts this way.

> *In his realm, the Beyonder was everything and everything was him . . .*
> *and he was content! But, by chance, an event in our universe opened*
> *a pinhole into his beyond-realm—and through the pinhole he glimpsed*
> *the Earth! For the first time in his existence he became curious! So, he*
> *began to observe! For years he watched the Earth! One thing con-*
> *founded him above all else— this incompleteness. Beings of our uni-*
> *verse seemed to have—this thing called—desire! He set about to study*
> *it! He sought subjects! His eye, naturally was caught by beings of great*
> *powers, presence. . . and palpable desire!*

> * * *

> *The Beyonder chose only a handful of beings from among hundreds*
> *he'd observed—like candies from a tray! Some he simply seized . . .*
> *some he merely opened the door for—and they came of their own free*

will! Those ones, I heard, really puzzled him—I mean, can you imagine a total outsider trying to make sense of the way superheroes behave? Once he had his subjects, he sorted them according to the nature of their desires!

That's the backstory to *Secret Wars*, one of the most popular battle miniseries in the Marvel Universe until too many of us just had to see what was in the *Civil War* miniseries. The Beyonder sets up this arena battle for his own reasons, and motivates both sides with the promise of big rewards.

The Supreme Power—Or Not

Before they hear the challenge, they all witness the destruction of an entire galaxy and the construction of the planet where they will do battle. The battle planet is created from the pieces of planets brought from the destroyed galaxy as well as some other galaxies, and even from pieces of a Denver suburb on Earth. Even the mighty ego of Dr. Doom is humbled.

> *Awe-inspiring . . . humbling . . . feats dwarfing the wildest imaginings of the gods! The power necessary . . . it's incalculable . . . inconceivable!*

While they are still standing around picking up their jaws, the promise, the challenge - the prize for the winner is announced along with the terms by the Beyonder.

> *I am from beyond! Slay your enemies and all you desire shall be yours! Nothing you dream of is impossible for me to accomplish!*

Before the appearance of the Beyonder, Galactus was one of the supreme powers in the Marvel Universe. Along with other entities like Eternity, he possessed the Power Cosmic, a sort of ultimate tricked out atomic energy wielded on a cosmic scale. He was the planet eater, the destroyer of worlds, the ultimate cosmic gourmand. Even though he came close to death a couple of times, he was revived or returned, and reigned as the undisputed king of the power pyramid for many years because Eternity rarely showed up and the Living Tribunal was busy with other universes. But then the Beyonder showed up and kidnapped him, placing him with bad guys such as the Enchantress, Ultron, the Molecule Man, Dr. Octopus, and Dr. Doom to name a few.

After seeing the Beyonder's display of power, no wonder they all believe him. Even Galactus believes the almost unbelievable claim of the Beyonder; he's just not willing to wait. Because he's one of Marvel's supreme powers in the universe, Galactus is used to getting his way, especially after a full meal. So he goes front man, ignoring the others, and gets blasted.

> *You! Beyonder! Hear me! Hear Galactus! I sense that you are truly a being from beyond this universe—this multiverse! I sense the energies you wield . . . and I know . . . I KNOW—! You can take from Galactus, devourer of worlds, his Hunger! You can end his ceaseless, monstrous craving for the very essence of living worlds—! Let it be DONE! I will not wait! I will not let some petty charade delay my respite! The torment must end NOW!*

Galactus just wants an end to his eating disorder, and he thinks the Beyonder can do it. However, he doesn't recognize that the Beyonder is more powerful than he is, otherwise he wouldn't feel that he could demand immediate satisfaction. Maybe there are other powers that the Beyonder can provide, but what kind or how much?

There are obviously different kinds of powers. The dramatic richness of the Marvel Universe is a combination of different kinds of power and different degrees of those powers. The main combatants in the story lines usually have just one or two powers that are very different from the powers of the others. The drama and the excitement is in how all these powers play out in battle. Which brings us back to that old adage—*it's not what you've got it's how you use it* that counts. Maybe "how-you-use-what-you-have" can be a talent or power too. Consider some examples of Marvel villains' powers.

Take Magneto, the super mutant bad guy perpetually causing trouble for Professor X and his band of good mutants. His mutant ability makes him master of electromagnetic fields and forces. A genius, he knows genetics, engineering, and technology Sort of like Tony Stark gone over to the dark side. He lifts submarines and oil tankers or anything else of the metal persuasion. If you saw the movie "X-Men: The Last Stand," he moved the Golden Gate Bridge so the mutants under his command could traverse it to assault Alcatraz Island.

The Lizard, on the other hand, has the abilities of a super reptile (as imagined by Marvel): ability to scale walls, super speed and agility, great strength and a strong deadly tail. Molecule Man controls all non-living matter down to the molecular level; Klaw commands and is actually composed of sound. We could go on, but you get the idea: powers are diverse, their uses equally so. No one has it all, and where supervillains are concerned, there's never enough.

How Much Is Enough?

With all these guys on the road to Oz to ask the wizard (in this case the Beyonder) for enough power to rule the universe, it makes sense to wonder how much is enough? If they can get enough, they can rule the Universe and live happily ever after, or maybe even win the power lottery and become all-powerful—omnipotent, as the philosophers say. At least some of the major villains believe this—especially Dr. Doom. Most of his cohorts—like the rest of us—want more money, more fame, a nice house, friends, maybe even a relationship, but Doom wants it all.

> *We—we have seen the power to end and begin universes . . . and you dwell on cheap lust for your selfish desires?*

Doom wants the real thing, not just bragging rights. You can tell because he's got this the habit of calling himself all-powerful in situations like *Fantastic Four* #50, when he lifts the powers of the Silver Surfer.

> *Now, it is I who possess the cosmic power which once was his! Never before has any one human being been as totally supreme—as invincibly superior—as I! Now let mankind beware—for Doctor Doom has attained powers without limit—power enough to challenge Galactus himself!*

Doom believed it was possible to just keep gaining power until he was all-powerful, but all his bragging was silenced instantly when he ran into the "cosmic dog fence" Galactus left to keep the Silver Surfer on Earth. Doom wasn't even close to challenging Galactus, and we know that neither was the Silver Surfer, Hollywood notwithstanding.

The point is, no matter how many kinds of powers Doom adds, there might be another kind of power he hasn't added yet. Some new creature in some far distant universe, or merely a new comic book writer with an even greater imagination might create a power unknown before. This could go on forever as new writers discover new powers. It seems to happen whenever we go where no man has gone before. If you can *always* find another power, then that means there is an infinite number of them.

The same thing would apply to degrees of power. If you can always increase your degree of power, notch it up a little, make it a little stronger, then there are a lot of levels above you—an infinite number in fact. That in turn means that no matter what level you're at (unless you've started with omnipotence) there are infinite levels of power above you. That's an interesting thing for us infinity-challenged mortals who are used to finite conceptions of power. If there actually are infinite levels in the picture, is there even a top level that counts as omnipotence? We'll get to that soon, but let's return to our candidate for omnipotence.

Doom has a big task ahead of him if he's going to grind his way to the top. He's going to have to work as hard as any of us would, even Galactus, since we now know the Beyonder is far above him. Professor X notes that *"To the Beyonder, even Galactus is less than a Fly . . ."* Doom feels the same way, *"Power so great . . . it humbles us! We are . . . bacteria . . . dust . . ."*

Doom, Galactus, or any of us would have to add an *infinite* amount of power to call ourselves all-powerful or omnipotent. That means if you don't start out at the top (let's face it, none of us does), you won't get there by addition since you'd have to spend an infinite amount of time adding power to achieve your goal. Galactus would have to spend an infinite amount of time consuming an infinite number of worlds. That's the crazy thing about infinity, no matter how much power you gain, you'll never get any closer to omnipotence—the top level—unless you find a way to make the move in just one step. Adding more is certainly having more, but it's not infinite.

In Search of All-Powerful (With Doom Close Behind)

We are familiar with power in politics, in business, and in war. Doom, like many of us, knows he's low on the cosmic totem pole. He wants to get to the top, but we now know he won't get there the way he's going about it. However, Doom has decided that the

Beyonder is all-powerful or omnipotent, and true to his character, *"If there is power to be had, Doom must have it!"* Eventually Doom does just that, gaining the power of the Beyonder himself.

> *The Beyonder is dead—and the power which once was his is now mine! I, Victor von Doom, am the mightiest being in this . . . or any universe! I could destroy you all with a thought . . .*
>
> * * *
>
> *By the dark gods! My least whim alters the world around me! Such is the power coursing within me that stone and steel are wisps of nothing which bend and transform in slavish obedience to my merest stray thought!*

But what can he actually do now? The Beyonder was going to fulfill all desires and grant all wishes. Now that Doom has the Beyonder's power, what can he do?

The Impossible Is Beyond the All-Powerful

First, let's be very picky and consider whether the Beyonder can actually do whatever we ask. Anything we ask can be put into words and arranged into a written sentence. So what if we ask the big B to make a purple Hulk? Better yet, let's ask him to make us a spherical cube. Could he do it? Those are two different shapes— spheres and cubes—and it's necessary to the meaning of the words and the concepts of spherical and cube that they are different. So how could something be both spherical and cube shaped?

You might say that one end could be spherical and the other cube shaped, but that's not what we asked of the Beyonder. We asked for a spherical cube, and although it's possible for us to put those two words in a sentence, we nonetheless can't even conceive of what we're asking for. The way we think about spheres and cubes *requires* that they couldn't be the same object.

So even if the Beyonder is omnipotent, he can't do the impossible. Even if we put the request in a carefully formed sentence, he couldn't create things that couldn't in principle exist. That goes for Dr. Doom as well. We all may wish for the impossible, but even an omnipotent being can't make the impossible happen. We could distract ourselves for a long time trying to decide what's impossible and what's not, but the point is that if any task is impossible (like spherical cubes), then that is a task beyond the Beyonder, Galactus, or the cosmically-poweful Dr. Doom.[1]

Fortunately there's an easy way to identify the whole class of actions that would be impossible for the all-powerful. We can recognize an impossible action by its description. They all have a similar sound—a stone too heavy to lift, a tree too tall to climb, a pancake too big to flip, and so on. The logic goes like this: if we say an all-powerful being can make one of these, then there is something else she can't do, namely, lift the stone, climb the tree, or flip the pancake. If we say that she can't make them, then that's also something she can't do. Either way there is something the Beyonder, and any omnipotent being, can't do. Even if that doesn't fit with our intuitive conception of omnipotence, it nonetheless *must* be true that they cannot do it. Omnipotence cannot perform feats of logical impossibility, though that still leaves the wide realm of the possible in its place. What's safe to say is that if something *can* be done, then omnipotence can do it.

Let's leave that aside for a moment because there's a more basic worry nearby. If one of our villains intends to ask the Beyonder to make him all-powerful, is that even possible? Assume for the moment that the Beyonder is all-powerful. Doom wants to be more powerful than the Beyonder because he doesn't like being second best, but you can't really be all-powerful if another being is more powerful than you are. That would mean there was something the other being could do that you couldn't. This is just a truism in logic since you wouldn't be the highest ranked, and we've already seen that there isn't a level just below Omnipotence because that pesky infinity thing won't allow it. So if the Beyonder couldn't make Doom a "more powerful, all-powerful" being, then maybe Doom could settle for equality. Is that an open possibility?

It Might Be Lonely at the Top

If both Galactus and Beyonder gained infinite power, Galactus would no longer need to feed and the Beyonder would no longer need to consume galaxies as snacks and wonder about desire. Both

---

[1] People debate whether this would similarly limit Chuck Norris, but in deference to the focus of this volume and our fear of roundhouse kicks, we will refrain from any assertions of fact in regards to Mr. Norris's abilities.

would be all-powerful, able to affect any part of the universe or multiverse in any way they wished. We already know that neither of them could do the impossible, like adorn themselves with spherical cubes. However, as long as they didn't try to oppose one another at the same time there probably wouldn't be any contradictions or paradoxes. That said, accidents happen, especially when Doom is busy trying to steal their powers.

Let's say that an omnipotent Galactus has decided to fly straight home for lunch and ignore the non-Euclidean aspects of space and the fact that he turned his home into energy in *Secret Wars*. Suppose also that the omnipotent Beyonder decides to only allow circular flight. What would Galactus's flight path be? If Galactus flies straight home, he flies in a circle because the Beyonder's omnipotence requires it, but when Galactus decides to fly straight his omnipotence insures that he will. Who wins?

If either does, then the other is not all-powerful, and if they both fail, then neither is omnipotent. They both can't win because (ignoring non-Euclidean space again) you can't fly in a circle and a straight line at the same time. That would be impossible, and we now know that even omnipotent beings can't do the impossible. Really, it seems the only way they can avoid this paradox is to avoid disagreeing. They must both be in complete agreement, or at least one of them mustn't care about the flight path.

It's hard to see villains who have spent their lives not co-operating trying to be better and agreeing to co-operate. On the other hand, they often seem to co-operate adequately enough to fight the heroes in *Secret Wars*. So, maybe they would agree to divide up the multiverse with each of them being the only omnipotent being in a given universe. That they could do *almost* anything they wanted within their separate domains.

All Desire Is Drama

We have spent some time looking at the most powerful beings in the Marvel Universe, especially the ones that are constantly calling themselves all-powerful, and we've discovered that it's unlikely that any of them actually *is* all-powerful or omnipotent. Once you start exploring what it means to be all-powerful—and some of the limits of omnipotence—it's easier to appreciate the vast possibilities out there in the multiverse. We might even begin to feel that once you become all-powerful, you have a different agenda than you had before. You no longer care about climbing the corporate ladder, or being the richest person on earth.

Even Doom seems to have an epiphany when he thinks he's got it all. He should have known what we know now, that the very act of stealing omnipotence meant that what he was getting wasn't it. Stealing the Beyonder's power implies at least that the Beyonder lacks at least the power to safeguard his own omnipotence. Thus, any power that Doom was able to steal would leave him infinitely short of the top level. Alas, he just never seems to learn.

> *Now, I am all-powerful! I have nothing to prove to lesser creatures—and none are my equal! I am complete . . . serene in my omnipotence! The dark, seething desires which once drove and shaped Doom are no more! Nothing in this universe—nothing of which you can conceive, no matter how cosmic in scope—could possibly merit my attention! For as eternity is to you . . . I am to Eternity! I have transcended all concerns of this plane of existence.*

In the Marvel Universe (and in our own) getting what you want means starting from a position where your reach exceeds your grasp because "getting" means the object of your desire is separate from you. But for any omnipotent being, there can be no separation between its desires (if it they can actually be said to have any) and their fulfillment because that would suggest a deficiency. An omnipotent Galactus needn't fly straight home, he could just be there. Flying takes time, which means it's possible we could make a lunch date he couldn't meet. That in turn allows that an omnipotent Galactus could try to get to a lunch date that he couldn't meet, and the nature of omnipotence makes that impossible. In the Marvel Universe the drama of the story demands battle and struggle, and perhaps the greatest proof that any character *isn't* all-powerful (whether in the story or in our real life) is that they need to engage in the drama or struggle in the first place.

17
What's Venom's Poison?

JOHN MATTHEWSON and DAVID WALL

Venom stands out as a supervillain because of its complexity: it is a fusion of human host and alien symbiote that lives on the host's adrenaline and emotions. This symbiote causes its hosts to do things they would not otherwise have done, in two different ways. First, it gives them abilities such as incredible strength and the ability to change appearance—the symbiote makes its hosts *super*. Second, it causes them to perform actions they themselves would normally find objectionable—it makes its hosts into *villains*.

It's the second of these that interests us here, because it raises a number of questions: are Venom's hosts responsible for their actions? If they are *made* into villains, are they really villains? And if they *are* responsible for their actions, to what extent are they responsible?

Your Hosts

The symbiote half of Venom is from another planet, where it was ostracised by its own kind because it didn't want to kill its hosts. In *Secret Wars*, Spider-Man accidentally released the alien from its containment unit, and when it covered him like a new black and white outfit, Spider-Man initially thought that the symbiote was just an alternative suit.[1] Although this "suit" made Spider-Man more powerful than usual, he eventually realized that it was actually feeding on his emotions, and was even making him do things in

---

[1] See *Secret Wars* (December 1984).

his sleep without his knowledge. Reed Richards (Mr Fantastic of the Fantastic Four) helped free Spider-Man from the alien's grip. This greatly upset the symbiote because it had formed a powerful connection with Spider-Man, almost like a love scorned![2] This connection was so strong that the symbiote retained Spider-Man's powers and eventually passed them to any of its new hosts.

The first and most famous of these was Eddie Brock. Brock was originally a successful reporter, but after claiming the wrong guy was responsible for a number of murders, he lost his job, the respect of his colleges, and eventually his wife in a painful divorce. Brock blamed all of this on Spider-Man, who had brought in the real culprit. When the symbiote found him, it recognized a hatred of Spider-Man similar to its own. With Brock's consent, the symbiote bonded with him, giving him all of Spider-Man's abilities, plus massive strength and the symbiote's own ability to shape-shift. These powers, driven by the shared wish to pursue a single-minded vendetta against the web-slinger, made Venom one of Spider-Man's greatest foes.

Brock has always revelled in the difficulties and dangers he inflicts on Spider-Man, but he is not a completely reprehensible character. Although he wants to harm Spidey, Brock also wants to protect the innocent, and often uses his powers as Venom to act as a vigilante. In some cases, this desire has been powerful enough to motivate him to work alongside Spider-Man to save innocent people from harm.

Strangely enough, the symbiote's third host was Brock's ex-wife, Anne Weying. In *Venom: Sinner Takes All #3*, Weying lay unconscious and dying from a gunshot wound when the symbiote saved her life by bonding with her. Together they went on to slaughter the people they thought responsible for her shooting, but when Weying later separated from the symbiote she was horrified and disgusted by what had occurred. Her ongoing feelings of guilt and seeing Brock return as Venom eventually contributed to her committing suicide.

Brock and his wife have dramatically different experiences of Venom, yet when they perform their villainous acts as part of Venom, they seem to be in similar situations. Each acts violently in

---

[2] See *Amazing Spider-Man #317* (Michelinie and McFarlane) for an example of this weird attraction.

a way they wouldn't have if they had not been bonded with the symbiote. However, we might reach contrasting verdicts about how responsible each is for their actions. Eddie Brock's story is (mostly) the story of a villain, but Weying's is (mostly) the story of a victim. Is there an important difference in the moral responsibility borne by these two hosts as Venom?

Whence Great Responsibility?

A traditional view of moral responsibility says that someone can only be morally responsible for a particular action if it was possible for him or her to have done otherwise.[3] On the face of it, this seems right: it would indeed be strange to hold someone responsible for doing something they had no choice about. Unfortunately, this won't help us explain why Venom's hosts have different levels of responsibility. Both Brock and Weying are manipulated in the same way by the symbiote. So if the symbiote makes its host unable to avoid doing evil, its influence would excuse both Weying *and* Brock from responsibility for their actions. Alternatively, if the symbiote doesn't affect its host's ability to do otherwise, then it won't excuse either of them. Thus, the traditional view of moral responsibility doesn't track our intuition that some distinction could be made between Brock and Weying as Venom.

However, there are good reasons to think the traditional view is wrong. Most famously, the philosopher Harry Frankfurt described a kind of case that appears to be a counter example to the view.[4] In these *Frankfurt cases*, a person performs a particular action according to his or her beliefs and desires in the normal way, even though they could not have done otherwise. Consider Eddie Brock's case: he bonded with the symbiote voluntarily because of his desire for revenge on Spider-Man and his belief that the symbiote could help him accomplish it. But suppose that unbeknownst to Brock, if he hadn't done this willingly, the symbiote would have forcibly bonded with him anyway. In that case Brock couldn't have avoided becoming Venom. Still, the symbiote didn't *actually* have to do this; Brock bonded with it for his own reasons, and it seems

---

[3] This is what's known as the 'principle of alternative possibilities'. M. McKenna, "Compatibilism," *Stanford Encyclopedia of Philosophy Online*, 2004.

[4] H. Frankfurt, "Alternate Possibilities and Moral Responsibility," *Journal of Philosophy* 66 (1969).

that he is thereby responsible for doing so, even if he couldn't have done otherwise. So it looks like the traditional, "must have been able to do otherwise" view is false. So what does moral responsibility depend on, and how can it reconcile our different intuitions about Brock and Weying?

The Sources of Venom

Maybe we can make sense of this by focusing in on Eddie Brock. Why do we think that Brock would be responsible for becoming Venom *even if* he couldn't have avoided doing so, as we just supposed? It seems that the *way* in which he became Venom is crucial: Brock bonded with the symbiote due to his own beliefs and desires in the normal way. The idea that whether someone is responsible for their actions is determined by how their actions were actually produced is called *Source Compatibilism*. According to source compatibilism, if someone is the source of their actions in the right way, then they are said to have *guidance control* over their actions, and they are therefore responsible for those actions.[5]

Philosophers differ over what exactly is the "right way" for a person to be the source of his or her own actions, but perhaps the most popular view is the one proposed by philosophers such as Robert Nozick, Daniel Dennett, and John Martin Fischer.[6] To understand their view, let's start by thinking again of Brock's bonding with the symbiote. This involved only a few aspects of his psychology, such as his desire to have revenge on Spider-Man and his belief that he could do so by bonding with the symbiote. But it didn't involve things like his belief that you can get great hot-dogs from the vendor at the bottom of his apartment block. Importantly, it didn't actually involve any forceful interference by the symbiote because, as it happened, Brock reached the decision on his own.

According to Fischer, guidance control over an action requires that the psychological features actually involved in causing that

---

[5] McKenna, "Compatibilism."

[6] Robert Nozick, *Philosophical Explanations*, Harvard University Press, 1981; Daniel Dennett, *Elbow Room: Varieties of Free Will Worth Wanting*, MIT Press, 1984; J.M. Fischer, *The Metaphysics of Free Will*, Blackwell, 1994; J.M. Fischer, "Responsiveness and Moral Responsibility," in *Responsibility, Character, and the Emotions*, Cambridge University Press, 1987; J.M. Fisher and M. Ravizza, *Responsibility and Control: An Essay on Moral Responsibility*, Cambridge University Press, 1998.

action are *responsive to reasons* to an appropriate extent. Usually, a person's actions depend on the reasons they have for taking those actions, and so a change in those reasons would normally result in a change in their actions. For example, suppose Brock had been very afraid of the symbiote, or discovered that Spider-Man hadn't intended to cause him misery. In that case he might not have willingly bonded with the symbiote. The fact that the psychological factors underlying Brock's decision to bond with the symbiote might have lead him to choose differently, had he had such different reasons for action, means those factors are appropriately responsive to reasons. On this view, it doesn't matter whether the symbiote would have bonded with Brock forcefully if he didn't choose to for himself. What's relevant are just those features that were *actually* involved in his action. In the case of Brock's bonding with the symbiote, his revenge motive and beliefs about the symbiote's powers were responsive to reasons, so he did have guidance control and therefore responsibility for that action.

Can this idea explain our different verdicts about Brock's and Weying's responsibility for their villainous deeds? If so, we need to identify what psychological features are involved in their actions while each was Venom. Here things get complicated because Venom's actions have their source in both the host *and* the symbiote, which means they're not based on the host's psychological features in the normal way.

The Tangled Web We Weave

When bonded with the symbiote, the hosts do things that they wouldn't normally do. Weying is horrified at what she did as part of Venom, but Brock points out that "the suit can't make you do anything you don't want to do."[7] Though Weying finds what she did disgusting, somewhere inside herself she *wanted* to kill those people. So we have two apparently conflicting pieces of information. On the one hand, the symbiote can't make you do what you don't want to do. On the other, the symbiote makes you do things that you wouldn't normally do; sometimes even things that you might hate. How can we resolve this conflict?

In one sense, having conflicting desires is actually quite familiar. When desires clash we typically weigh up their respective

---

[7] *Venom: Sinner Takes All #3* (October 1995)

strengths, sometimes consciously deliberating and sometimes without reflection, and act on the stronger desire. Normally, Weying's desire not to murder would have prevented her from killing her assailants, even if part of her "really wanted" to kill them. So how did the symbiote bring her to act on her weaker desire?

The simplest way would be if Venom just acted on a mixture of both their respective, individual desires. Both Weying and the symbiote hated Weying's assailants, but while she desired *not* to physically hurt them, the symbiote desired just that. The collective agent that is Venom would therefore have three relevant desires: the desire for revenge (from Weying and the symbiote), the desire to kill (from the symbiote) and the desire not to be a murderer (from Weying). If the symbiote's desire to kill was more powerful than Weying's desire not to be a murderer, then Venom, the fusion of them both, would end up with its overall strongest desire being to kill, and thereby act on that desire. But remember Brock's point about the symbiote's limits. If the fusion's actions are just a matter of the relative strengths of the desires of each individual, then the symbiote could make the host do things they had *no* desire to do, just by having a stronger desire. Part of the reason Weying is so distraught is because she knows that deep down, she really *did* want to kill the men. So the simplest account isn't quite right.

A different way that Venom's actions might have their source in both host and symbiote is if, rather than introducing its own desires, the symbiote suppresses some of the host's desires to get what it wants. In this way, the symbiote has an influence on how the host acts without making them do things they have no desire to do. So perhaps the symbiote inhibits Weying's desire to not kill, which then allows her desire for retribution to come to the fore. Bonding with the symbiote might thus be similar to being under the influence of alcohol, drugs, extreme anger, or some other disruption of your usual inhibitions. This would fit nicely with what we know about the symbiote's thriving on emotions and adrenaline—it doesn't *want* its host to resist their most basic urges!

While the symbiote's influence might be similar to having too much alcohol or losing your temper, how it brings about that result is quite different. Unlike alcohol, drugs, or intense emotions, the symbiote *chooses* how to wield its influence. It deliberately picks out particular desires that will deliver the emotional outputs that it wants, and it interferes with the host's psychology to insulate these features from contrary considerations. In effect it changes the set of psychological features that determine the host's actions. It is no longer the host's beliefs and desires, but rather her adjusted and insulated beliefs and desires that determine Venom's action. For this reason the symbiote genuinely bears at least some of the blame for Venom's actions.

The Weight of Weying's Sins

Let's work with the theory that when someone fuses with the symbiote to become Venom, it suppresses at least some of their normal desires in order to make them act in potentially villainous ways. Recall that according to the reasons-responsiveness view, in order to be accountable for your actions, those actions must be caused by features of your psychology that are appropriately responsive to reasons. When Weying is part of Venom, this is missing because of the symbiote's interference. The set of psychological features that actually causes her actions is not merely her natural desire for revenge (along with relevant beliefs). Instead it is that desire insulated against contrary considerations. That would mean Weying acted from a psychological feature that isn't responsive to reasons, which means she therefore didn't have guidance control over Venom's villainous actions and thus isn't entirely responsible for them. Does Weying nonetheless share some degree of responsibility?

It's plausible that responsibility comes in degrees. Someone might be more or less responsible for an action rather than simply responsible or not. Perhaps there was some sense in which Weying could have resisted the symbiote to disengage its interference. After all, Spider-Man doesn't become a villain when he bonds with the symbiote, and he remains a hero throughout *Secret Wars* and afterwards.[8] On the other hand, if you need to be a veteran superhero to be able to resist the symbiote's influence, then can we really hold an ordinary person like Weying ultimately responsible if she succumbs?

Perhaps Weying is blameworthy for having even some small desire to kill her assailants, but this would be only a minimal amount of blame. After all, it's a very rare person who doesn't have *any* malevolent desires that they should probably keep in check. It probably wouldn't take too much work to think of something you

---

[8] Thanks to Ben Dyer and Chris Miller for pointing out this difference.

have briefly considered or imagined doing that you quickly realised would have been quite wrong! The real pity is that Weying was unable to see that her responsibility was so minimal. If she had, she might have avoided taking her own life.

Brock Hangs in the Balance

These ideas about moral responsibility and how the symbiote has its influence seem to explain our verdict about Weying, but can they explain the difference between Weying and Brock as well? We might think they can't. After all, the way in which the symbiote influences its host's actions is the same for Brock as it is for Weying, and so our reasoning should be the same. Before he bonded with the symbiote, Brock presumably had the same beliefs and desires that everyone has that prevent them from murdering others. Whatever these were, the symbiote insulated them from Brock's desire to kill Spider-Man so that his reasons-insensitive desire to do so would instead determine how he would act.

The framework plausibly explains much of Brock's other behavior as Venom. He typically does not intentionally harm innocents, which makes sense if Brock simply has no desire to harm anyone other than Spider-Man. In that case, there would be no relevant desires for the symbiote to selectively insulate to bring about such harm.

However, the psychological features that cause Brock's actions are just as unresponsive to reasons as Weying's. So just as we allowed earlier that Weying isn't entirely responsible for her actions, then it might seem that Brock isn't either. However, Brock and Weying are different in two important respects. In stark contrast to Weying's negative response, much of the time, Brock is *happy* with what he does as Venom. He *endorses* his villainous actions, while Weying rejects hers. Furthermore, Brock *voluntarily* bonded with the symbiote in full knowledge of how this would influence his subsequent actions. In effect, Brock showed a *higher level* of guidance control because the psychological features that led him to bond with the symbiote were responsive to reasons, even though his *later* actions became insensitive to reasons once he became Venom.

In this way, we can think of Brock as making Venom's way of acting his own, and this makes him accountable for actions that come about in this perverse way. This is why we judge him more responsible than Weying. She does not endorse the symbiote's adjustment of her psychology, so she cannot be fully responsible for Venom's subsequent actions.

A Complex Supervillain

Venom's complexity makes it a particularly cool supervillain, but also a particularly interesting one philosophically. The symbiote and host comprise a collective in which the psychologies of both are involved in determining how it acts. The hosts are not mere marionettes being manipulated by the symbiote, but neither is the symbiote an indiscriminate or passive influence on them.

Now we can see that Venom's hosts suffer from a kind of moral misfortune: although they do bad things, it's not entirely their fault. However, as Brock demonstrates, Venom's hosts can become complicit in, and therefore responsible for, the evils committed by Venom. Perhaps that is how the real villains are revealed.[9]

---

[9] Thanks to Stella Bolaki, Brett Calcott, Kirsty Douglas, Ben Dyer, Patrick Forber, Ben Fraser, Ole Koksvik, Holly Lawford-Smith, Hatha McDivitt, Chris Miller, Rose Miller, Jean Stace, Kim Sterelny, and Chris Wall for helpful discussion and comments on earlier drafts.

18

Drawing a Line in the Sandman

TIM PICKAVANCE

With the ability to make giant brick-fists and have punches just pass straight through him, the Sandman's composed of some pretty weird stuff.[1] I'll call that stuff *mansand* because whatever else it is, it isn't ordinary sand. *Mansand* is a freak combination of irradiated sand and human genetics, though the details we're given about what *mansand* exactly is are a bit sketchy.

Uncovering that mystery would be interesting for a physicist or a biologist perhaps, but as a philosopher I'm interested in a puzzle of identity raised by the very existence of *mansand*. When is some *mansand* the Sandman? The question may sound bizarre, but notice that not just any old collection of *mansand* gets you the Sandman because he regularly leaves bits of *mansand* behind. Witness Peter Parker's boot-full of *mansand* in *Spider-Man 3*, or the large amount strewn about on the street any time he does battle with the Sandman. That *mansand* is decidedly *not* the Sandman.

So what? you (rhetorically) ask, *that little boot-full of mansand certainly isn't* big *or* complex *enough to be Sandman, and his remains just aren't* arranged *in the right way.* Fair enough, but this response implicitly assumes an answer to the question: some *mansand* is the Sandman if there's enough of it and it's arranged in a suitably complex way. We'll see in a bit that although this is a natural way to respond, it generates a rather tricky puzzle that has no obvious solution. Nonetheless, there's a serious question here

---

[1] Just to keep everything straight, the Sandman we're interested in here is the Spider-Man villain, not Neil Gaiman's character from the Vertigo series of the same name.

for the Sandman and any other supervillain (or hero) who can
become (or just is) composed of a particular element or material.
Should these characters worry about what will happen to them if
their component substance is blown apart or scattered? Which parts
identify the Sandman as an individual if all parts are functionally
the same? (A version of this thought applies to a question we might
have about Wolverine, Sabretooth, and other super-healers: if
Wolverine gets blown apart, why don't all the parts regenerate into
several versions of Wolverine?) Whatever the right story is about the
identity of the Sandman will probably also inform us about characters like Clayface, Emma Frost, some versions of Iceman,
Colossus, and maybe even Dr. Manhattan (of *Watchmen* fame),
though he at least seems to have no trouble reconstituting himself
since it was the first trick he learned.

Much of the day-to-day workings of our lives and our society
turn on whether *this* thing is the very same thing—is identical to—
that thing. Identity can have different meanings. Contrast the sense
of identity at work in the following sentences:

**1. He's just not the same person anymore: he used to be
so sweet and loving, and now he's angry and cruel.**

**2. You look so different that it's hard to believe—though
I know it's true—that you're the same daughter that I haven't
seen for forty years!**

The first sentence refers to identity as a kind of expression of our
changing personality, but notice that it assumes that we're talking
about the same person as both loving and cruel. By contrast, the
second sentence wonders at, and affirms, the thing the first sentence assumes: personal identity picks out a particular individual
that endures through change. The second sense is the one we're
interested in, and here's an example of how important it is in everyday life. The propriety of our system of justice turns on our ability
to make true judgments of identity, and we think it is morally
wrong to punish an innocent person for someone else's crimes!

So how is it that people can endure through at least some
changes? Coming up with an answer requires that we understand a
thing's relationship to its parts, and if we're wrong about how this
works, then the underpinnings of Sandman's identity will slip
through our fingers.

Fine-Grained Distinctions

One of the many ways that things change is through the gain and loss of their parts, and we normally don't think such changes generate separate individual entities. Not too long ago my wife and I moved from Austin, Texas to Fullerton, California. We were fortunate enough to have movers do the heavy lifting, but they managed to take a chunk out of the face of our mahogany dresser in the process. Although the dresser lost a part, we wouldn't normally think it ceased to exist and that we now owned a separate dresser just because we lacked the missing part. We own the very same dresser that we owned before that chunk was gouged from its face. So says common sense, anyway.

The same goes for human beings. A couple of years ago, my wife's father had a hip replacement. Even though Lyle emerged from the surgery with a new titanium hip joint, he was nonetheless the same person. He didn't undetectably die and get replaced with Bionic-Lyle on the operating table. (Anyway if he did, Bionic-Lyle certainly gets as frustrated with the Cubs as Lyle used to!) In the Sandman's case, we normally think that when he leaves bits of *mansand* scattered around New York, whether in Peter Parker's boot or in the subway or on the street, the self-same Sandman survives. He can lose some of the *mansand* that composes him without ceasing to exist.

We can capture these ordinary intuitions about endurance through change as a general, highly plausible principle:

PART EXCHANGE: If object *o* has *the x*s as parts but not *the y*s, then *o* can lose insignificant numbers of *the x*s or gain insignificant numbers of *the y*s without ceasing to be *o*.

PART EXCHANGE is the first piece of our puzzle. PART EXCHANGE just captures our normal assumption that things can gain and lose parts without ceasing to be the thing that they are. So if you find yourself puzzled by its precise formulation, no worries; just remember that normal assumption. It's easy to get hung up on the unusual locutions "*the x*s" and "*the y*s," but these are just a way to refer all at once to more than one thing. Such "plural referring devices," phrases that refer all at once to more than one thing, are actually quite common. In sentences like, "The boys lifted the piano," "The legs of the table are sturdy," and "The astronauts formed a semi-circle to have their picture taken," "the boys," "the legs," and "the astronauts" are plural referers. In PART EXCHANGE, "*the x*s" and "*the y*s" are plural references to whatever parts an object happens to have, and to some things that aren't parts of an object, but which are possible for the object to have as parts. "*The x*s" and "*the y*s" are just an abstract placeholder for an object's parts (or possible parts) in the same way that "*o*" is a placeholder for the object.

In the case of the Sandman, PART EXCHANGE works in the following way. Suppose that we divide up the world's *mansand* into two groups: that *mansand* that is part of the Sandman and that *mansand* that he leaves behind. In that case, "*o*" refers to the Sandman; "*the x*s" to the *mansand* that's part of him; and "*the y*s" to the *mansand* that isn't part of him. What PART EXCHANGE tells us, then, is that the Sandman could lose some bits of *mansand* that are currently part of him without ceasing to be himself, and furthermore that he could gain some bits of *mansand* that aren't currently part of him without ceasing to be himself. This is as we should expect, and matches our usual assumptions about my desk and that chunk of mahogany and Lyle and his new titanium hip.

The second piece of our puzzle begins to take shape when one considers some further observations about ordinary objects. Consider the book you're holding. The book has a number of parts: it's composed of sheets of paper, some ink, and some glue. These bits of paper, ink, and glue are *all* the parts (we can suppose) of the book. The book, in other words, is constituted by that paper, ink, and glue. This is a natural judgment that expresses what we might call a "materialist" view of the book. It's natural to think that the book is nothing more than the sum of its material parts, the collection of paper, ink, and glue. After all, what more to the book could there be than paper, ink, and glue? What part of the book is left out of that list?

Even if we have all the parts, they can't be related to one another in just any old way. The pages need to be in the right order, the glue in the right place, the ink distributed to produce the right arrangement of letters and words and so on. If I shred the book into a trillion tiny pieces and scatter the resulting bits of paper, ink, and glue around Lake Michigan, there's no book left over. Nonetheless, the sum of those bits still exists, even if it is now just highly scattered, like a galaxy or all the world's Christians. But books aren't like galaxies or groups of people. They require a certain order or arrangement to their parts. So, besides the parts as such, there is the arrangement of the parts, and the arrangement must be recognized in our view about the identity of the book. Now we can improve our view of the book's basic composition: the book is nothing more than the sum of its parts when those parts are arranged appropriately.

This adjustment is consistent with the materialist view we've tentatively taken about the book. The arrangement of the world's material parts is an aspect of the material description of the world, and the materialist view of the book is driven fundamentally by the claim that a complete description of the material aspects of the world will include a complete description of the book.

Most philosophers these days, and I would conjecture most non-philosophers, take a materialist view of living beings as well. On top of embracing materialism about books and chairs and cars and stars, this would mean that birds and dogs and whales and people are material objects as well. In that case, we could capture these common intuitions about both inanimate objects and living beings in a principle like the following.

> MATERIALISM: If object *o* has *the xs* and nothing but *the xs* as parts, then there is nothing more to *o* over and above *the xs* and their arrangements: when *the x*s are arranged appropriately, they constitute *o*.

Let's suppose that's right. If MATERIALISM is true for living things as well as non-living things, then as a living being, the Sandman is a wholly material thing. So how does that advance our understanding of the Sandman's identity?

Let's return to our initial question. We initially wanted to know what makes some *mansand* battle residue while other *mansand* is the Sandman? *Materialism* implies that some *mansand* is the Sandman whenever that *mansand* is arranged in the appropriate way. So we have at least a partial answer to the question with which we began. The partial answer is that if some particular bits of *mansand* are all of the Sandman's parts at some time arranged in a particular way, then whenever you have that particular *mansand* in that particular arrangement, you have the Sandman himself.

This was, if you remember, very much like our initial response to the question about when *mansand* is the Sandman, but it's also different in an important way. The view of identity that emerges from MATERIALISM is more stringent than our initial response because it requires that some *particular mansand* be arranged in the right way. Not that just *any old mansand* will do. Our initial response implied that you get the Sandman when you have enough *mansand, any mansand*, arranged in the right way. By contrast, MATERIALISM imposes an extra requirement: it's only when you have some *particular mansand* arranged in some *particular* way that you are committed to the claim that you have the Sandman. A commitment to MATERIALISM, then, is a commitment to less than one is committed to given the initial response. A more stringent principle makes for a weaker commitment, since it applies to fewer cases.

Unfortunately, if we accept both PART EXCHANGE and MATERIALISM, then we are forced to accept something crazy.

Norman Osborn's Sandman Plan

Suppose Norman Osborn came to be fixated on the Sandman as part of a plan to make his own private army of Sandmen. The plan is to create this army by duplicating the Sandman many times over. Somehow Osborn comes to know enough about the Sandman that he can tell you exactly how many particles of *mansand* compose the Sandman at some time in the past and what their precise arrangements were then. Let's call the collection of *mansand* that composed the Sandman on May 3rd the *Maysand*. Now imagine that after May 3rd, as the Sandman wreaks havoc on New York, Osborn goes about collecting all the *mansand* that the Sandman leaves behind, and that was a part of the Sandman at that earlier time. Remember that according to PART EXCHANGE, the Sandman survives the loss of these small quantities of *mansand*, even though he probably loses a lot of it over time. Eventually, the Sandman replaces all the *Maysand* with new *mansand*. Every bit of the *Maysand* is left behind and collected by Osborn, who then proceeds to arrange it just the way it was on May 3rd.

Here's where the puzzle emerges. According to MATERIALISM, Osborn has made something that is identical to the Sandman. This is so because MATERIALISM tells us that the Sandman is nothing over and above the sum of properly arranged *Maysand*. But remember, the Sandman is also out wreaking havoc on New York! It's not clear which thing is properly the Sandman, and now he's wreaking havoc on our intuitions as well!

Here we have the puzzle squarely before us. PART EXCHANGE allows for the Sandman to slowly lose all of the *Maysand*, which in turn makes it possible for the *Maysand* to be reconstituted by

Osborn. On the other hand, MATERIALISM says that Osborn's reconstituted thing must be the Sandman, even though the Sandman has been wreaking havoc on New York in an unbroken rampage since May 3rd as well. Thus we have the possibility that two things are identical to one thing, and that, my friends, is just crazy. It's logically impossible for two things to be one thing.

Let me assure you that this is no mere trick of the dialectic, but a puzzle that has existed since Plato first identified it using the Ship of Theseus as his example. The ship of Theseus is a legendary Athenian ship on which the Greek hero Theseus (the slayer of the Minotaur for you mythology buffs) returned from Crete. As Plutarch weaves the myth, the Athenians worked hard to preserve the ship, replacing plank after plank with new wood as the original planks deteriorated. You can probably guess how the puzzle works here as well.

1. Replace each plank, one at a time, noting that PART EXCHANGE implies that the Ship of Theseus survives any single plank replacement.

2. Reassemble the old planks, noting that MATERIALISM implies that the Ship of Theseus is present wherever the old planks are present in their old arrangement.

3. Note, therefore, that we now have two things, not one, whereas if both PART EXCHANGE and MATERIALISM are true, we should have one.

This puzzle is just like the one with the Sandman constructed above. In the place of the Sandman, we have the Ship of Theseus. In the place of the *Maysand*, we have the planks. In the place of Osborn, we have some crazy Athenians. In both cases, we have two things that are supposed to be one. So in both cases, swallowing both PART EXCHANGE and MATERIALISM is doing the impossible.

Drawing a Line in the Sand

We face a choice now that the puzzle is before us: to make sense of the Sandman's relationship to his constituent parts, one of the principles has to go. We must give up either *part exchange* or *materialism*. I find *part exchange* more compelling than *materialism*, because the latter requires me to think that things cannot endure through any change of their parts. That is quite a sacrifice! I would seemingly have to deny that Spider-Man endures the spinning of a single web, or that my wife endured through her last haircut! Maybe you could modify MATERIALISM so that it does not play its part in generating the puzzle. However, doing so without sacrificing the intuitive force behind MATERIALISM is, if you will allow me an understatement, rather difficult.

Have we really gone any distance toward answering the question with which we began? Exactly when *is* some *mansand* the Sandman? At least we can say that we've uncovered one way *not* to make progress toward that destination! Our initial response collapsed on reflection; some *mansand* is *not* the Sandman if you've got it arranged in a suitable way because things other than the Sandman can satisfy that condition. Further, it's no good to impose the further constraint, captured by MATERIALISM, that you must have some *particular mansand* arranged in some *particular* way. But where does that leave the Sandman? What substantive alternatives are there?

There's a long tradition of thinkers, going back at least to Plato and Aristotle, through Thomas Aquinas and Descartes, to contemporary philosophers like Alvin Plantinga and Richard Swinburne, who believe that a person's material parts aren't all there is to the person. The Sandman, on the sort of view defended by this tradition, is more than some *mansand* arranged in the right way. The Sandman also has an immaterial part, a part which itself has no proper parts. Because these views see the person as a functional whole comprised of material and immaterial parts (the immaterial bit usually being identified as a "soul" or "spirit"), the view these philosophers share in common has been called "dualism." For the dualist, a person's identity is dependent on the continued existence of their indivisible soul, not on the arrangement of their particular (and divisible) material parts.

How does opting for "dualistic" persons—persons with a material aspect and an immaterial aspect—help with the puzzle? Well, if a person's identity through change, including the exchange of parts, depends on the identity of that person's soul rather than his or her body, then the challenge posed by *part exchange* is no challenge at all because one's soul has no parts to gain or lose! In the Sandman's case, some *mansand* is the Sandman just in case the *mansand* in question is properly related to the Sandman's soul. The upshot is that when Osborn reconstitutes the *Maysands* to build his private army, he doesn't get the Sandman himself because the *Maysand* is no longer related in the right way to the Sandman's soul.

That said, I don't want to leave you thinking the road traveled by dualists is smoothly paved. Dualists owe an account of what the "proper relation" is between the Sandman's (and any other person's!) material parts and his (or her) immaterial part. Furthermore, they owe a more general account of the relationship between the Sandman's soul and body. How would the dual entities that comprise the Sandman causally interact? The nature of that interaction is at least an apparent mystery, given just what I've said so far. Can dualism be generalized from persons to other animals, plants, and inanimate objects? What makes something immaterial, rather than material; that is, what is it for something to be immaterial? These are pressing questions for the dualist. Unless answers to these questions and others of their ilk are forthcoming, dualism will seem less and less promising and will be less a substantive alternative than a suggested possibility. So the real upshot for comic book fans is that there's loads more work to do if we want to understand how Sandman relates to his *mansand*, how we relate to our bodies, and more generally how things relate to their parts. At the very least, the Sandman himself has some soul-searching of his own to do.

19
Brainiac's Brain, Brainiac's Body

PAUL LOADER

Once upon a time (1958 to be precise), DC created a comic book character called Brainiac. A skinny little green guy from another planet, Brainiac was something of a loner, drifting around the universe shrinking cities and putting them in bottles for his own private amusement. His only companion was a monkey called Koko, a rather sad looking creature to whom he would address the occasional remark about evil schemes.

Then something happened in the universe outside of Brainiac's universe, the universe of legal writs and product sales. It turned out that in the real world there was something else on the market named Brainiac. Edmund C Berkeley, a pioneer in the fields of computer science and robotics, was marketing a product called the Brainiac Computer Kit, an educational toy that enabled you to fiddle with pieces of circuitry in order to solve rudimentary logical problems or play tic-tac-toe.

The Brainiac Computer Kit had been marketed before Brainiac the supervillain had come onto the scene, and although there was no suggestion that DC had deliberately stolen the name, Berkeley still objected to its continual use for a character unrelated to his gizmo. After some wrangling, a compromise was reached. It was decided that DC could carry on having a supervillain called Brainiac provided that he was reinvented as a computer and provided that this reinvention was accompanied by some publicity for the Brainiac Computer Kit. Thus it was that, six years after his first appearance, Brainiac became a computer. Here's how it happened in *Superman* 167 (1964).

Brainiac's Origin

Lex Luthor, Superman's arch enemy, has at his disposal a sophisticated piece of hardware called a Time-Space Thought Scanner. This equipment can "tune into minds in any part of the universe and in any period of time" and Luthor uses this device to search for the most powerful mind that has ever existed in the universe. This turns out not to be Aristotle or Hegel but rather the mind of a "Master Computer" built on a distant planet. Luthor peers into the past to follow the story of this computer and finds that it was built with good intentions by green-skinned "human" scientists who hoped to take advantage of its increased intellect. "A human mind is a sixth level effector" whereas their new creation "is built to be a tenth-level effector."

However, things tend to go awry where silver age comics and computers are concerned. Soon there's a whole generation of these master computers and when they decide that they've had enough of being subservient to humans, they proceed to enslave the planet. Nor does their ambition stop there. Soon "the mechanical minds make plans to rule other worlds." They hope to achieve this by constructing a human-looking computer that they can send off to other worlds as a kind of spy. He'll "case the joint" and then they can invade.

At first, the master computers are a little undecided about just how intelligent they should make the new android, for they realise that if they wire his circuits in a particular way he could become a "twelfth order mind" more intelligent than they. They eventually decide against this policy on the quite reasonable grounds that he might try to enslave them if given a superior mind. What one wonders, of course, is why the master computers don't rewire themselves in such a way—but they must have their reasons.

This new computer, then, is Brainiac, a revelation which is accompanied in the comic by a footnote stating "Brainiac is also a trademark registered by Berkeley Enterprises Inc., manufacturers of the famous Brainiac Computer Kit." It turns out, according to the revamped storyline, that Brainiac has known all along that he is a computer but has been following instructions from the master computer to "pretend to be human in every way!" This rather bizarre turn of events is nevertheless useful for us—for Brainiac's reinvention as a humanoid computer raises interesting questions about artificial intelligence and just what it means to be "brainy" in the first place.

Would Brainiac Be Brainy?

The reconstruction of Brainiac as a computer was in some respects a more than merely random event. The late 1950s onwards had seen a growth of interest in the possibilities offered by computers, and in a new area of research calling itself Artificial Intelligence, or "AI." The orthodoxy shared by many involved in this field was that computers had the potential to become genuinely intelligent, that they could do anything that a human mind could do. Brainiac's reincarnation was a product of this time and a reflection of popular interest in a new idea.

This leads us to our main question: just how intelligent could Brainiac really be? Some readers might think this a slightly suspect question—rather like asking "if ducks could talk, would they sound like Donald Duck?" Brainiac is, after all, a fictional character, and as far as I know, no DC comic contains a detailed blueprint for his design.[1] Nevertheless, comic book writers and AI researchers at the time tended to hold in common certain popular assumptions about mind and intelligence which, along with the state of available technology, dictated the direction of AI research and imposed limitations on its success. Insofar as Brainiac embodied these assumptions we can get some idea of what his limitations should be.

What kind of assumptions are we talking about? Well one of them might be summarized as follows:

1. Being intelligent is mainly about thinking logically and having lots of facts at one's disposal.

This is a view which, in the words of the philosopher Andy Clark, imagines mind "as a kind of combination logic machine and filing cabinet." Translated into a program for AI design, it implies creating a system which can store as much data as possible and which has the ability to manipulate that data in accordance with programmed logical rules.

We can find suggestions of such an approach in various Brainiac storylines. For example, the notion that intelligence is held to be

---

[1] I say this with some trepidation for it is entirely possible that a reader with encyclopaedic knowledge of DC comics will direct me to an obscure and overlooked issue of *Super Team Family* containing sixteen pages of programming code!

dependent on the quantity of data storable is made explicit in Brainiac's revised origin story. At one point in *Superman* 167, the Master Computers look down disdainfully at the humans they have managed to enslave and declare "These humans with their poor sixth-level minds and limited memory banks do not labor fast enough." It is unclear why exactly having limited memory banks should be connected to not working hard enough. Perhaps the writer's own logic circuits were having a holiday that day, but the point for our purposes is clear. Human intelligence is felt to be inferior to that of the Master Computers because of their inability to store enough data. Clearly then, the intelligence installed in the Master Computers' subsequent creation—Brainiac—is superior partly because it is capable of storing of much larger quantities of data than a human brain.

Likewise we might note that there are a plethora of incidents and remarks which drive home the message that artificial intelligence is all about thinking logically or making difficult calculations. When Jimmy Olsen is installed with a Brainiac type brain in *Jimmy Olsen* 86, the main advantage it confers on him is that of being able to calculate the grains of sand in an anthill and predict the winner of a horse race. "I've studied the nags themselves," Jimmy says, "now I'll feed all the statistical factors about them into my memory banks."

In another episode (*Superman* 271), when Superman attacks Brainiac's flying saucer, Brainiac's thought bubble reads "He shook my flier with that blow . . . but my calculations show that in desperation he is beginning to panic . . . so it would be logical for me to go outside and give him a reason to panic!" This turns out to be a set-up on Superman's part, and when Superman emerges victorious, he hurls Brainiac into deep space with the lesson that "the human brain under stress . . . is superior to any computer."

Arghh! It's the Frame Problem!

Is Superman right? What's wrong with facts and logic? His parting remark about the performance of the human brain under stress— although in fact reflecting a generalized sentiment concerning the limitations of any computer system—does point us in the direction of a critique of the "logic machine and filing cabinet" approach to intelligence. This critique is well illustrated by a story told by the philosopher Daniel Dennett involving several of Brainiac's under-achieving cousins.

Suppose a robot has the general task of "fending for itself" and learns that its precious spare battery is in a room also containing a time bomb. The robot locates the room and finds that the battery is on a wagon. He is able to deduce that removing the wagon will result in the battery being removed from the room before the bomb explodes and so he removes the wagon. Unfortunately the bomb is also on the wagon, and so the robot removes both, and is blown to smithereens. Back to the drawing board!

What the robot needs when it formulates its plans, the designers decide, is not just awareness of the intended implications of its actions (for example, that the battery will be out of the room before the bomb goes off) but also "the implications about their side effects" (for instance, that if the bomb also comes out of the room then the robot will be blown to smithereens). They thus build a new robot with this capability. This robot also hits upon the plan of pulling the wagon out of the room. However this time it pauses to consider all possible side effects- that pulling the wagon out of the room will not change the colors of the walls of the room, that it will cause the wheels to revolve more times than there are wheels on the wagon, and so on through an unending list of possible side effects. While it's doing so, the bomb explodes, and the new robot is also blown to smithereens.

Finally the designers decide to build a third robot that can tell the difference between relevant and irrelevant implications, but this task of categorizing side effects as relevant or irrelevant turns out to be just as unending and once again the robot is blown to pieces.

Dennett's story illustrates what is known as the Frame Problem—although there's some disagreement about what the Frame Problem actually is. Some regard it as a mere technical difficulty once faced by traditional AI,[2] but others see it as a more general philosophical problem. How does anyone (machine or human) manage to plan an action in a world of infinite detail and ongoing change? Why aren't we like Dennett's robot, paralysed by consideration of all possible consequences of our actions every time we decide to do something? As Dennett puts it, "How do we look before we leap?" One answer, suggested by philosopher Hubert Dreyfus, is that there is an essential difference between human

---

[2] Very roughly, the problem of how to represent in logic the consequences of an action without generating a lot of irrelevant non-consequences.

intelligence and that of artificial creatures which try to get by using facts and rules. The everyday intelligent activity of human beings cannot be understood as the result of detached logical thinking and exhaustive consideration of facts:

> If we construe our everyday understanding as based on knowledge of facts, our everyday skills look like impossible feats.

(Readers who want to know *why* Dreyfus thought that human intelligent behavior could not be based on knowledge of facts and rules should look at his book, *What Computers Still Can't Do*.)

Artificial Dumbness

So where does this leave Brainiac? Despite Superman's jibe about the superiority of the human brain, Brainiac strangely does not appear to have any particular problem dealing with the real world. It's true that he is often depicted as lacking human insight. For example in *Superman* 167, Brainiac has been locked in a cage by Superman and is unable to devise a plan of escape. Lex Luthor appears and instructs him to start a fire in his cage. Brainiac takes his advice, and when the fire is detected by a sensor the gate opens automatically, allowing him to escape. Luthor explains that this was predictable because Superman would not allow a prisoner to die in a cage. "Why didn't I ever think of that?" wonders Brainiac, and Luthor replies, "you didn't think of it because you don't know human psychology . . ." But this flaw in Brainiac's reasoning capacities is scarcely comparable with the sheer dumbness of Dennett's robots—if Brainiac had suffered from the Frame Problem, he would probably have remained in the cage even after Luthor started the fire.

Likewise it is true that Brainiac is consistently outwitted by human (or Kryptonian) intelligence. Indeed, considering that intelligence is his selling point it's sometimes surprising how easily Brainiac is outwitted. In *World's Finest Comics* 144, Superman is lying face down on the floor after a series of events involving rocks and a Kryptonite-infected Jimmy Olsen. Brainiac concludes he must be dead and charges towards him exclaiming, "I did it. I finally destroyed Superman!" Superman then jumps up and catches Brainiac. "Sorry to disappoint you," he says, "I was only pretending to be dead!" Ah, the old "pretending to be dead" ruse. However Brainiac's weakness here is less indicative of the limitations of his programming than it is of his being a villain in a *Superman* comic aimed at young readers.[3]

Just a No Body

Mishaps aside, it is a little mysterious how Brainiac manages to engage with the world as successfully as he does, given that his design exemplifies a "facts and logic" approach to intelligence. The mystery deepens when we consider that he also seems to exemplify a second assumption of traditional AI about mind and intelligence:

2. Being intelligent has little to do with having a body

This principle complements the previous one. If intelligence is just about storing facts and thinking logically, then one does not set great store on the importance of a body. Although thinkers, human or machine, need a body to house their thinking unit (the brain), the body's role in intelligence itself is at best peripheral. A robot would need some means of inputting information from the world (artificial eyes or ears) and then, once an action has been decided upon, some means of outputting actions to the world (maybe wheels or artificial arms). The thinking itself takes place between the perceiving and acting, and in a distinct physical location.

Some commentators have argued that traditional AI's commitment to this kind of disembodied intelligence betrays its roots in a "Cartesian" approach to mind—the approach found in the work of the philosopher René Descartes (1596–1650). Descartes, like traditional AI theorists, also reduced intelligent human activity to the activity of thinking, famously describing himself as "a thing that thinks" and making thought the defining characteristic of mind. He likewise showed a general disregard for the role of the body in intelligent behaviour. Mind, on Descartes's analysis, was an immaterial substance or a soul. It was not "extended in length, breadth and depth" and did not "participate in anything that pertains to the body." AI researchers did not subscribe to the literal separation of

---

[3] This applies particularly to *World's Finest Comics*, which was aimed at younger readers.

mind and body in this metaphysical way, but the principled separation of mind stuff and body stuff is the same.

So, why are we suggesting that Brainiac's intelligence is of this "disembodied" sort? He evidently has a quite sophisticated humanoid body after all, and seems quite comfortable in it. However, notice that Brainiac's intelligence remains unaffected by the type of body he has or even whether he has much of a body at all. This is evident from the outset. When the master computers are putting Brainiac together they make it clear that Brainiac's human appearance is only for the purpose of disguise. The fact that he has a humanoid form—eyes that rotate, fingers that waggle, and legs that run and jump—is not held to contribute one iota to the type of intelligence or mind that he has. "We must give him human mannerisms or he'll be suspected" say the master computers, but these mannerisms are just a cover for his real existence as a logic processor. Brainiac and the master computers have identical brain units, it just so happens that one is installed in a humanoid body whereas the others are installed in contraptions resembling washing machines with arms.

This point is underlined in various Silver Age 'brain transplant' stories. We have already mentioned how Brainiac installs a Brainiac brain in Jimmy Olsen, but this story was typical of a whole raft of stories during that period. Brainiac brains were also installed in a female robot (*Worlds Finest* 164) and even in Superman himself (*Jimmy Olsen* 130). What such episodes tell us is that the Brainiac type brain is a self-contained, portable entity that can be hooked up to any kind of device irrespective of body type or component materials. It's a conception of intelligence confined to the brain, and in principle detachable from any bodily goings-on.

I Act, therefore I Think[4]

Again readers might be wondering why there's a problem with the second assumption of traditional AI—what has intelligence got to do with the body after all? Dreyfus suggests an answer:

> What distinguishes persons from machines, no matter how cleverly constructed, is not a detached, universal, immaterial soul but an involved, situated, material body.

---

[4] The motto of the University of Wisconsin's Laboratory of Embodied Cognition.

Of course there are many other things that distinguish us from machines—such as not being on sale for $199 at PC World—but Dreyfus is here making the anti-Cartesian point that our "involved, situated, material body" is integral to our intelligence.

Taking Dreyfus's lead, philosophers and AI researchers have developed this point in a variety of ways. Some have called into question the idea, alluded to earlier, that intelligent behavior is best understood in terms of a sequence which begins with perception and ends with action, with cognition (roughly "thinking") occurring somewhere in the middle. It's partly this sequence which has justified the relegation of the body to a secondary role in intelligent behaviour. The alternative suggestion is that perception, cognition and action are much more closely intertwined.

A simple example is provided by philosopher Andy Clark. Imagine playing Tetris, a computer game that involves rotating falling shapes so that they slot into spaces at the bottom of the screen. One way of describing our engagement with this game would be in terms of the perception, cognition, action sequence. First we perceive the position and orientation of a falling shape, then we mentally calculate how the shape should be rotated, then we rotate the shape in accordance with our calculations. This would be the disembodied Brainiac-style approach. All the thinking is done between the perceiving and the acting. Indeed we can imagine that, in this particular instance, Brainiac might excel at the task by plugging his brain directly into the console and dispensing with use of his body altogether.

However the perception–cognition–action sequence does not bear much resemblance to what human beings actually do. We are more likely to rotate the shape on the screen until it looks right and then let it drop into the slot. The cognition stage does not take place in separation from our rotating the shape—we might even say that our thinking is partly constituted by our rotating the shape on the screen. At the very least, our thinking, perceiving and acting are tightly bound together. Our rotating of the shape, itself facilitated by our tracking the shape with our eyes and fiddling with the buttons on the controller, is central to our decision making. In short, we use our bodies to help us arrive at a solution.

Other philosophers have suggested that it is not just the having of a body but the type of body had which affects how we think about the world. Lakoff and Johnson point out how many of the concepts we use to understand and reason about the world are metaphorical in nature. These metaphors, in turn, are often derived from the orientation of the human body in physical space. Thus the structure of much of our reasoning is ultimately based on the structure of the human body. Take the concept of future events. Future events are often conceived of as ahead of us in some metaphorical sense. This, it might be conjectured, is because human beings have one pair of eyes on the front of their head and tend to walk in the direction that their eyes are looking. If, like some comic book alien, we had eyes on all sides of our head we might start thinking of future events as surrounding us, which would certainly have a big impact on the way we reasoned about the future!

These arguments, and many others we haven't mentioned, are all aimed at undermining the prejudice that being clever is what the brain does, and the body is just there for burping, farting and getting us from A to B. Although they do not imply that a robot can never be clever in the way that human beings are, they do lessen the likelihood that Brainiac, with his disembodied intelligence, would have been able to exhibit the human-like intelligence we usually associate with him.

The Last Panel

And so we reach the last panel of our story "Brainiac's Brain, Brainiac's Body." En route Brainiac has encountered formidable foes such as the Frightful Frame Problem and the Embodiment Gang. How should we summarise this epic saga? Perhaps by returning to the beginning.

Once upon a time there was a little green guy called Brainiac who was transformed into a disembodied facts and logic machine. As a result, he would most likely have become less intelligent rather than more so.

The Rogue's Gallery

KIRBY ARINDER, in the months following his contribution to this volume, has pursued a steady recovery. He has been placed in a quiet position as Adjunct Instructor of philosophy at VMI, where he can be kept under the gentle, careful watch (and deadly accurate guns) of the Virginia Commonwealth Militia. His nerves are delicate still (he bursts into sobs at the mention of Joseph Milton's name or, inexplicably, at the sight of a Red Lobster), but physicians assure us that he shall avoid a relapse into madness, provided his research can be kept to philosophies exoteric, and not too ancient. Though tight-lipped about his current projects, Dr. Arinder assures us that "something great is coming, a thing of dark beauty and power."

ROBERT ARP has a Ph.D. in Philosophy from Saint Louis University and has interests in Philosophy of Biology, Informatics Ontology, and the Philosophy of Pop Culture. His most recent books include *Scenario Visualization: An Evolutionary Account of Creative Problem Solving* and an edited anthology with Alex Rosenberg titled *Philosophy of Biology: An Anthology*. At present, he works as an ontologist for The Analysis Group, LLC doing contract work for the US Department of Defense. He could tell you exactly what he is working on, but then he'd have to kill you.

LIBBY BARRINGER is pursuing her Ph.D. in Political Theory at the University of California, Los Angeles. She received her B.A. from the College of William and Mary in Virginia, and a Masters in Political Theory from the London School of Economics. Interested in taking over the world from a young age, she was drawn to political philosophy when she realized that Plato had some pretty useful thoughts on the

subject. When not busy asserting her Will to Power or torturing innocents with the finer intricacies of utopian theory, she spends her free
time cooking up ways to feed her ninja henchman army, polishing
swords, and cackling to herself. Other villainous credentials include a
vague knowledge of martial arts, a utility belt, and a tendency to brood.

BEN DYER completed his first M.A. in Philosophy at Biola University in
2003, and has since acquired another at Bowling Green State
University in Ohio. He is currently completing his Ph.D. in Applied
Philosophy at the latter institution in an attempt to rectify an unfortunate confusion stemming from his unquenchable thirst for power and
the misleading order of the academic titles "master" and "doctor." In
the interim, he has taught courses in applied ethics, philosophy, and
religious studies. His latest ~~master~~ doctor plan involves political obligation (to him of course) and will be unleashed upon the world in
2011.

GALEN FORESMAN is an Assistant Professor at North Carolina Agricultural
and Technical State University. In addition to his many duties as a
teacher and faculty member he's a Senior Fellow at the Villainy Self
Improvement Center, where he's most well known for his pocket man-
uals, *Three Steps to Laughing Maniacally* and *How to Wring Your
Hands So People Know You're Up to No Good*.

RAFAELA HILLERBRAND is a lapsed physicist, head of the research group,
Ethics for Energy Technology, and professor at the department of philosophy at RWTH Aachen University. She completed a Ph.D. in philosophy and another in theoretical physics when she realized after
extensive studies of Calvin and Hobbes that she had become a math
atheist. As surplus physics seemed for tigers, she turned to philosophy
instead and now tries to square both subjects by working on philosophy of science.

NOAH LEVIN, who has the trivial mutant power of an iron stomach
(which, despite his arguments in his chapter, he does think makes him
superior to non-mutants), is an Instructor/Graduate Student at Bowling
Green State University. He is just beginning what will hopefully be a
long and illustrious career, beginning with this publication. He does
work primarily in the areas of computers ethics and bioethics, arguing
that everything be given its due moral consideration . . . except for
henchman. They're expendable.

CRAIG LINDAHL-URBEN earned a B.A. in philosophy at Reed College, and
somehow realized that Socrates didn't have a Ph.D. and getting one

would be superfluous for living a wise and full life. Currently trying to decide whether to watch the lightning at night or the road it illuminates, he has spent many years in the computer industry, both owning a computer software company, and as an executive for large computer companies. He was formerly Publisher and Editor-in-Chief of a weekly newspaper which is almost like being all-powerful if you've got the same view of things as Dr. Doom.

PAUL LOADER has been researching a PhD. in Philosophy of Cognitive Science for several millennia at Sussex University. His research interests include Marxian themes in cognitive science, Wittgensteinian critiques of cognitive science, and philosophy of parapsychology. He thinks the real supervillains are mainly to be found running countries and large corporations, but rumors abound that he is even now raising an army of sentient robots to set matters aright.

JOHN MATTHEWSON is a postgraduate student at the Australian National University. His primary philosophical interests are the medical sciences and population biology. His favorite supervillain is Mister Quimper from The Invisibles. John plans to have his own evil empire one day, but he is currently too busy writing a dissertation, playing video games, and being a dad. He considers his co-author David Wall to be the first recruit to this empire, but Dave seems a bit confused about this.

JOSEPH MILTON, despite the warnings of Kirby Arinder that it was the dangerous product of a mind poisoned by a hubris so great as to rival that of Prometheus punished, yes, eternally by the Gods for bringing the *power* of fire to man in defiance of their holy decree, completed his MA thesis in philosophy at the University of Virginia. Now, scarred and sworn to revenge himself upon the whole of the world, he lives in New Orleans, studying the dark arts of capitalism as a graduate business student at Tulane University, tending his many cats, and waiting to see what arrives from "the fecund, muddy sea."

DANIEL MOSELEY, a.k.a. "Mr. Moseley," spends his days in and out of Arkham Asylum. Batman fights to put an end to Mr. Moseley's attempts to corrupt the minds of the youth of Gotham. Mr. Moseley, like the Joker, does not have any superpowers, but he uses his theatrical and philosophical skills to accomplish his devious plans. Mr. Moseley has published book reviews, newspaper articles and a professional article on philosophical issues related to mental illness. He has taught philosophy courses at the University of Virginia and James Madison University.

RON NOVY is Lecturer in Philosophy and the Humanities in the University College at the University of Central Arkansas as well as the freshman Academic Advisor for the College of Liberal Arts. Ron has written essays for *Batman and Philosophy* (2008) and *Iron Man and Philosophy* (2010). Known to students as the fearsome "Professor Illegible Red Pen," Dr. Novy isn't so much evil as simply misunderstood.

DENNIS O'NEIL graduated from St. Louis University around the turn of the 1960s and joined the Navy just in time to participate in the blockade of Cuba during the Cuban Missile Crisis. After leaving the service, he worked briefly in journalism, until fellow Missourian Roy Thomas facilitated his entry into Marvel Comics. Denny shortly moved on to Charlton, and then DC, where he would pen his most famous work. At DC, he revitalized *Justice League of America*, and brought social consciousness back to comics for the first time in decades with the groundbreaking *Green Lantern/Green Arrow* series. His work on Batman—first as writer, then as editor—returned that character to its dark, gothic roots and has influenced every bat-scribe since. Denny is semi-retired and lives in Nyack, New York, with his wife Marifran.

JOHN OSTRANDER began his career in comics in the early 1980s and has worked on several Marvel and DC titles including *Justice League*, *Batman*, *X-Men*, *Punisher*, *Firestorm*, *Martian Manhunter*, and *Bishop*. His most famous industry credits include the reinvention of the Spectre as an agent of divine wrath, the reinvention of former Batgirl Barbara Gordon as the information specialist Oracle, and the creation of the metahuman dirty dozen known as the Suicide Squad. John currently works on *Star Wars Legacy* for Dark Horse Comics and writes a regular column at ComicMix.com.

TIM PICKAVANCE, Assistant Professor of Philosophy at Biola University, is a recent Ph.D. from the University of Texas, Austin. If he has a superpower, it's judging Mexican food, particularly of the interior and Yucatecan varieties. Therefore, he would be deathly afraid of most supervillains. Lyle, his first and only child, isn't so skittish, but that's because he's too young to know any better. Give him some time. Tim's currently working on papers with strange titles, most of which he has plundered from his dissertation on some issues having to do with the problem of universals, and he hopes to publish these papers in obscure philosophy journals. His dashing wife, Jamie, isn't impressed either.

JARED POON received his M.A. in Philosophy at the University of Florida, and is currently working on his Ph.D at the University of

California, Davis. While his main research interest is meta-ethics, there is a special place in his heart for robots, spandex, and robots in spandex. In his free time, he enjoys modifying his two cats with various exotic-particle-emitting weaponry. In the summers, he teaches kids thinking skills (and secretly, Superheroics 101) at Logicmills in Singapore, which is also where his secret underwater base is located.

CHRISTOPHER ROBICHAUD is an Instructor in Public Policy at the Harvard Kennedy School of Government. He is completing his doctorate in philosophy at MIT. Having wasted years roaming the halls of the Infinite Corridor with the hope that an experiment gone awry would transform him into a superhero, Christopher has since decided to go the easier route and embrace supervillainy. That's right. He's becoming a consequentialist.

CRAIG ROUSSEAU conceived and drew our original cover art. His superhero comic-book credentials include *Impulse, Batman Beyond*, and issues of *Batman: Gotham Adventures*. He's also known for *Spider-Man Loves Mary Jane: Sophomore Season, X-Men First Class*, and *Iron Man and the Armor Wars*. He both drew and co-created (with Todd Dezago) *Todd and Craig's The Perhapanauts*. Sharing his surname with one of the great thinkers of the past, Craig is celebrated for his exciting work in the not-quite-so-philosophical *Harry Johnson* series. Visit him any time at www.craigrousseau.com.

ANDERS SANDBERG is a lapsed computational neuroscientist who now works at the Future of Humanity Institute, a part of the James Martin 21st Century School and the philosophy faculty of Oxford University. There he explains neuroscience to philosophers and writes papers with them about the ethics of improving humans. Philosophy gives him an excuse to research everything from the ethics of love potions and extending human lifespan to the technical details of how to scan human brains into computers. He is also studying how to plan for the *really* far future, extreme disasters, and how to think well when you know you can't trust your own brain. If he is kicked out of the philosophy department he will make science fiction book covers instead.

J.J. SYLVIA IV recently completed his philosophy M.A. at the University of Southern Mississippi. While writing his thesis, "The Epistemological Framework of Television as an Ethical Problem," he would often don a cape and pretend he was fighting Mojo. Unfortunately, a cape is a hindrance in the summer heat of Mississippi, so he had to give up his superhero aspirations and take the thesis seriously, likely casting him as a villain in the eyes of his reality-television loving introduction to philosophy students.

CHARLES TALIAFERRO, Professor of Philosophy at St. Olaf College, is the author or editor of eleven books, most recently *Evidence and Faith: Philosophy and Religion since the Seventeenth Century.* When he was a boy, he dreamed of fighting supervillians in a role like Robin and then, a little older, he thought being Batman was cool. Now, a little older still, he hopes that if you are a superhero who fights supervillans, you will contact him if you would like the services of a philosophically trained valet who would gladly answer to the name of "Alfred."

ANDREW TERJESEN is currently a visiting Assistant Professor at Rhodes College in Memphis, Tennessee. Previously, he held positions at Washington and Lee University and Austin College. A freak misinterpretation of David Hume (caused by that know-it-all Richards!) has left him permanently scarred and unable to deal with anything other than issues in moral psychology and the Scottish Enlightenment. Fortunately, this has not been a hindrance to his campaign of world domination the old-fashioned way, through essays like the one in this volume as well as in *The Onion and Philosophy, Anime and Philosophy,* and *Manga and Philosophy.*

DAVID WALL is a lecturer in philosophy at the University of Northampton. David's evil scheme is to use philosophy to manipulate an army of minions to punish the world for misuse of the expression "begging the question." He considers his co-author John Matthewson, whom he met while both were postgraduates at the Australian National University in Canberra, as his first such recruit. John, on the other hand, insists that David is just deceiving himself if he thinks he's anything more than a side-kick.

SEAN WALTERS is a mild-mannered teacher of high school English in Long Beach, Mississippi, by day. By night he studies to become a Master of Gifted Education in order to open his own villainy-fighting School for Gifted Youngsters. Though his students frequently compare him to a certain well known web-slinger, he assures them that heights are definitely not his thing.

Index